ant
CAMBRIDGE LIBRARY COLLECTION

Books of enduring scholarly value

English Men of Letters

In the 1870s, Macmillan publishers began to issue a series of books called 'English Men of Letters' – biographies of English writers by other English writers. The general editor of the series was the journalist, critic, politician, and supporter (and later biographer) of Gladstone, John Morley (1838–1923). The first volume published was Samuel Johnson, by Leslie Stephen (1878), and the first series (which continued until 1892) eventually consisted of 39 volumes. The aim was to provide a short introduction to each subject and his works, but also that the life should illuminate the works, and vice versa. All the subjects were men, as were all but one of the authors (Mrs Oliphant on Sheridan); and all but one (Hawthorne) were English or Irish. The subjects range chronologically from Chaucer to Thackeray and Dickens, and an important feature of the series is that many of the authors (Henry James on Hawthorne, Ward on Dickens) were discussing writers of the previous generation, and some (Trollope on Thackeray) had even known their subjects personally. The series exemplifies the British approach to literary biography and criticism at the end of the nineteenth century, and also reveals which authors were at that time regarded as canonical.

Fielding

At the outset of this book, published in the first 'English Men of Letters' series in 1883, the poet and author Austin Dobson (1840–1921) declares his intention to restrict himself to giving a 'purely biographical' account of the life of the lawyer, novelist and dramatist Henry Fielding (1707–54). Fielding is probably best remembered today for his novels *Joseph Andrews* and *The History of Tom Jones* (1749), but in his own day he was famous not only for his writings in many different genres but also for his work as an innovatory Justice of the Peace in London. Dobson recounts Fielding's life from his schooldays at Eton to the production of his first play, and his subsequent careers as a writer, magistrate and controversialist, until his death in Portugal (where he had travelled in the hope that the climate would improve his health) in October 1754.

T0381803

Fielding

Austin Dobson

CAMBRIDGE UNIVERSITY PRESS

Cambridge, New York, Melbourne, Madrid, Cape Town,
Singapore, São Paolo, Delhi, Tokyo, Mexico City

Published in the United States of America by Cambridge University Press, New York

www.cambridge.org
Information on this title: www.cambridge.org/9781108034548

© in this compilation Cambridge University Press 2011

This edition first published 1883
This digitally printed version 2011

ISBN 978-1-108-03454-8 Paperback

English Men of Letters

EDITED BY JOHN MORLEY

FIELDING

FIELDING

BY

AUSTIN DOBSON

London:
MACMILLAN AND CO.
1883.

PREFATORY NOTE.

FROM a critical point of view, the works of Fielding have received abundant examination at the hands of a long line of distinguished writers. Of these, the latest is by no means the least; and as Mr. Leslie Stephen's brilliant studies, in the recent *édition de luxe* and the *Cornhill Magazine,* are now in every one's hands, it is perhaps no more than a wise discretion which has prompted me to confine my attention more strictly to the purely biographical side of the subject. In the present memoir, therefore, I have made it my duty, primarily, to verify such scattered anecdotes respecting Fielding as have come down to us; to correct (I hope not obtrusively) a few mis-statements which have crept into previous accounts; and to add such supplementary details as I have been able to discover for myself.

In this task I have made use of the following authorities:—

I. Arthur Murphy's *Essay on the Life and Genius of Henry Fielding, Esq.* This was prefixed to the first collected edition of Fielding's works published by Andrew Millar in June 1762; and it continued for a long time to be the recognised authority for Fielding's life. It is possible that it fairly reproduces his personality, as presented by contemporary tradition; but it is misleading in its facts, and needlessly diffuse. Under pretence of respecting "the Manes of the dead," the writer seems to have found it pleasanter to fill his space with vagrant discussions on the "Middle Comedy of the Greeks" and the machinery of the *Rape of the Lock,* than to make the requisite biographical inquiries. This is the more to be deplored, because, in 1762, Fielding's widow, brother, and sister, as well as his friend Lyttelton, were still alive, and trustworthy information should have been procurable.

II. Watson's *Life of Henry Fielding, Esq.* This is usually to be found prefixed to a selection of Fielding's works issued at Edinburgh. It also appeared as a volume in 1807, although there is no copy of it in this form at the British Museum. It carries Murphy a little farther, and corrects him in some instances. But its author had clearly never even seen the *Miscellanies* of 1743, with their valuable Preface, for he speaks of them as one volume, and in apparent ignorance of their contents.

III. Sir Walter Scott's biographical sketch for Ballantyne's *Novelist's Library.* This was published in 1821; and is now included in the writer's *Miscellaneous Prose Works.* Sir Walter made no pretence to original research, and even spoke slightingly of this particular work; but it has all the charm of his practised and genial pen.

IV. Roscoe's Memoir, compiled for the one-volume edition of Fielding, published by Washbourne and others in 1840.

V. Thackeray's well-known lecture, in the *English Humourists of the Eighteenth Century,* 1853.

VI. *The Life of Henry Fielding; with Notices of his Writings, his Times, and his Contemporaries.* By Frederick Lawrence. 1855. This is an exceedingly painstaking book; and constitutes the first serious attempt at a biography. Its chief defect—as pointed out at the time of its appearance—is an ill-judged emulation of

Forster's *Goldsmith*. The author attempted to make Fielding a literary centre, which is impossible ; and the attempt has involved him in needless digressions. He is also not always careful to give chapter and verse for his statements.

VII. Thomas Keightley's papers *On the Life and Writings of Henry Fielding* in *Fraser's Magazine* for January and February 1858. These, prompted by Mr. Lawrence's book, are most valuable, if only for the author's frank distrust of his predecessors. They are the work of an enthusiast, and a very conscientious examiner. If, as reported, Mr. Keightley himself meditated a life of Fielding, it is much to be regretted that he never carried out his intention.

Upon the two last-mentioned works I have chiefly relied in the preparation of this study. I have freely availed myself of the material that both authors collected, verifying it always, and extending it wherever I could. Of my other sources of information—pamphlets, reviews, memoirs, and newspapers of the day—the list would be too long ; and sufficient references to them are generally given in the body of the text. I will only add that I think there is scarcely a quotation in these pages, however ascertained, which has not been compared with the original ; and, except where otherwise stated, all extracts from Fielding himself are taken from the first editions.

At this distance of time, new facts respecting a man of whom so little has been recorded require to be announced with considerable caution. Some definite additions to Fielding lore I have, however, been enabled to make. Thanks to the late Colonel J. L. Chester, who was engaged, only a few weeks before his death, in friendly investigations on my behalf, I am able to give, for the first time, the date and place of Fielding's second marriage, and the baptismal dates of all the children by that marriage, except the eldest. I

am also able to fix approximately the true period of his
love-affair with Miss Sarah Andrew.   From the original
assignment at South Kensington I have ascertained the
exact sum paid by Millar for *Joseph Andrews;* and in
chapter v. will be found a series of extracts from a
very interesting correspondence, which does not appear
to have been hitherto published, between Aaron Hill,
his daughters, and Richardson, respecting *Tom Jones.*
Although I cannot claim credit for the discovery, I
believe the present is also the first biography of
Fielding which entirely discredits the unlikely story of
his having been a stroller at Bartholomew Fair; and I
may also, I think, claim to have thrown some additional
light on Fielding's relations with the Cibbers, seeing
that the last critical essay upon the author of the
Apology, which I have met with, contains no reference to
Fielding at all.   For such minor novelties as the
passage from the *Universal Spectator* at p. 26, and the
account of the projected translation of Lucian at p. 163,
etc., the reader is referred to the book itself, where
these, and other waifs and strays, are duly indicated.
If, in my endeavour to secure what is freshest, I have at
the same time neglected a few stereotyped quotations,
which have hitherto seemed indispensable in writing of
Fielding, I trust I may be forgiven.

Brief as it is, the book has not been without its
obligations.   To Mr. R. F. Sketchley, Keeper of the
Dyce and Forster Collections at South Kensington, I am
indebted for reference to the Hill correspondence, and
for other kindly offices; to Mr. Frederick Locker for
permission to collate Fielding's last letter with the
original in his possession.   My thanks are also due to
Mr. R. Arthur Kinglake, J.P., of Taunton; to the Rev.
Edward Hale of Eton College, the Rev. G. C. Green
of Modbury, Devon, the Rev. W. S. Shaw of Twerton-
on-Avon, and Mr. Richard Garnett of the British
Museum.   Without some expression of gratitude to the

last mentioned, it would indeed be almost impossible to conclude any modern preface of this kind. If I have omitted the names of others who have been good enough to assist me, I must ask them to accept my acknowledgments although they are not specifically expressed.

EALING, *March* 1883.

CONTENTS.

FIELDING.

CHAPTER I.

EARLY YEARS—FIRST PLAYS.

LIKE his contemporary Smollett, Henry Fielding came of an ancient family, and might, in his Horatian moods, have traced his origin to Inachus. The lineage of the house of Denbigh, as given in Burke, fully justifies the splendid but sufficiently quoted eulogy of Gibbon. From that first Jeffrey of Hapsburgh, who came to England, *temp.* Henry III., and assumed the name of Fieldeng, or Filding, "from his father's pretensions to the dominions of Lauffenbourg and Rinfilding," the future novelist could boast a long line of illustrious ancestors. There was a Sir William Feilding killed at Tewkesbury, and a Sir Everard who commanded at Stoke. Another Sir William, a staunch Royalist, was created Earl of Denbigh, and died in fighting King Charles's battles. Of his two sons, the elder, Basil, who succeeded to the title, was a Parliamentarian, and served at Edgehill under Essex. George, his second son, was raised to the peerage of Ireland as Viscount Callan, with succession to the earldom of Desmond; and from this, the younger branch of the Denbigh family, Henry Fielding directly descended. The Earl of Des-

S   B

mond's fifth son, John, entered the Church, becoming
Canon of Salisbury and Chaplain to William III. By his
wife Bridget, daughter of Scipio Cockain, Esq., of Somerset, he had three sons and three daughters. Edmund, the
third son, was a soldier, who fought with distinction under
Marlborough. When about the age of thirty, he married Sarah, daughter of Sir Henry Gould, Knt., of Sharpham Park, near Glastonbury, in Somerset, and one of the
Judges of the King's Bench. These last were the parents
of the novelist, who was born at Sharpham Park on the
22d of April 1707. One of Dr. John Fielding's nieces,
it may here be added, married the first Duke of Kingston,
becoming the mother of Lady Mary Pierrepont, afterwards Lady Mary Wortley Montagu, who was thus Henry
Fielding's second cousin. She had, however, been born
in 1689, and was consequently some years his senior.

According to a pedigree given in Nichols (*History and
Antiquities of the County of Leicester*), Edmund Fielding
was only a lieutenant when he married; and it is even
not improbable (as Mr. Keightley conjectures from the
nearly secret union of *Lieutenant* Booth and Amelia in
the later novel) that the match may have been a stolen
one. At all events, the bride continued to reside at her
father's house; and the fact that Sir Henry Gould, by
his will made in March 1706, left his daughter £3000,
which was to be invested "in the purchase either of
a Church or Colledge lease, or of lands of Inheritance,"
for her sole use, her husband having "nothing to doe
with it," would seem (as Mr. Keightley suggests) to indicate a distrust of his military, and possibly impecunious,
son-in-law. This money, it is also important to remember, was to come to her children at her death. Sir

Henry Gould did not long survive the making of his will, and died in March 1710.[1] The Fieldings must then have removed to a small house at East Stour (now Stower), in Dorsetshire, where Sarah Fielding was born in the following November. It may be that this property was purchased with Mrs. Fielding's money; but information is wanting upon the subject. At East Stour, according to the extracts from the parish register given in Hutchins's *History of Dorset*, four children were born,—namely, Sarah, above mentioned, afterwards the authoress of *David Simple*, Anne, Beatrice, and another son, Edmund. Edmund, says Arthur Murphy, "was an officer in the marine service," and (adds Mr. Lawrence) "died young." Anne died at East Stour in August 1716. Of Beatrice nothing further is known. These would appear to have been all the children of Edmund Fielding by his first wife, although, as Sarah Fielding is styled on her monument at Bath the *second* daughter of General Fielding, it is not impossible that another daughter may have been born at Sharpham Park.

At East Stour the Fieldings certainly resided until April 1718, when Mrs. Fielding died, leaving her elder son a boy of not quite eleven years of age. How much longer the family remained there is unrecorded; but it is clear that a great part of Henry Fielding's childhood must have been spent by the "pleasant Banks of sweetly-winding Stour" which passes through it, and to which he subsequently refers in *Tom Jones*. His educa-

[1] Mr. Keightley, who seems to have seen the will, dates it—doubtless by a slip of the pen—May 1708. Reference to the original, however, now at Somerset House, shows the correct date to be March 8, 1706, before which time the marriage of Fielding's parents must therefore be placed.

tion during this time was confided to a certain Mr
Oliver, whom Lawrence designates the "family chaplain."
Keightley supposes that he was the curate of East
Stour; but Hutchins, a better authority than either, says
that he was the clergyman of Motcombe, a neighbouring village.   Of this gentleman, according to Murphy,
Parson Trulliber in *Joseph Andrews* is a "very humorous
and striking portrait."   It is certainly more humorous
than complimentary.

From Mr. Oliver's fostering care—and the result shows
that, whatever may have been the pig-dealing propen-
sities of Parson Trulliber, it was not entirely profitless—
Fielding was transferred to Eton.   When this took place
is not known; but at that time boys entered the school
much earlier than they do now, and it was probably not
long after his mother's death.   The Eton boys were then,
as at present, divided into collegers and oppidans.   There
are no registers of oppidans before the end of the last
century; but the Provost of Eton has been good enough
to search the college lists from 1715 to 1735, and there
is no record of any Henry Fielding, nor indeed of any
Fielding at all.   It may therefore be concluded that he
was an oppidan.   No particulars of his stay at Eton have
come down to us; but it is to be presumed Murphy's
statement that, "when he left the place, he was said to
be uncommonly versed in the Greek authors, and an
early master of the Latin classics," is not made without
foundation.[1]   We have also his own authority (in *Tom*

---

[1] Fielding's own words in the verses to Walpole some years later
scarcely go so far :—

> " *Tuscan* and *French* are in my Head ;
> *Latin* I write, and *Greek* I——read."

Jones) for supposing that he occasionally, if not frequently, sacrificed "with true *Spartan* devotion" at the "birchen Altar," of which a representation is to be found in Mr. Maxwell Lyte's history of the College. And it may fairly be inferred that he took part in the different sports and pastimes of the day, such as Conquering Lobs, Steal baggage, Chuck, Starecaps, and so forth. Nor does it need any strong effort of imagination to conclude that he bathed in "Sandy hole" or "Cuckow ware," attended the cock-fights in Bedford's Yard and the bull-baiting in Bachelor's Acre, drank mild punch at the "Christopher," and, no doubt, was occasionally brought back by Jack Cutler, "Pursuivant of Runaways," to make his explanations to Dr. Bland the Head-Master, or Francis Goode the Usher. Among his school-fellows were some who subsequently attained to high dignities in the State, and still remained his friends. Foremost of these was George Lyttelton, later the statesman and orator, who had already commenced poet as an Eton boy with his "Soliloquy of a Beauty in the Country." Another was the future Sir Charles Hanbury Williams, the wit and squib-writer, then known as Charles Hanbury only. A third was Thomas Winnington, for whom, in after years, Fielding fought hard with brain and pen when Tory scribblers assailed his memory. Of those who must be regarded as contemporaries merely, were William Pitt, the "Great Commoner," and yet greater Earl of Chatham; Henry Fox, Lord Holland; and Charles Pratt, Earl Camden. Gilbert West, the translator of Pindar, may also have been at Eton in Fielding's time, as he was only a year older, and was intimate with Lyttelton. Thomas Augustine Arne, again, famous in days to come as Dr. Arne, was

doubtless also at this date practising sedulously upon that
"miserable cracked common flute," with which tradition
avers he was wont to torment his school-fellows.   Gray
and Horace Walpole belong to a later period.

During his stay at Eton, Fielding had been rapidly
developing from a boy into a young man.   When he left
school it is impossible to say; but he was probably seven-
teen or eighteen years of age, and it is at this stage of
his career that must be fixed an occurrence which some
of his biographers place much farther on.   This is his
earliest recorded love-affair.   At Lyme Regis there resided a young lady, who, in addition to great personal
charms, had the advantage of being the only daughter
and heiress of one Solomon Andrew, deceased, a mer-
chant of considerable local reputation.   Lawrence says
that she was Fielding's cousin.   This may be so; but
the statement is unsupported by any authority.   It is
certain, however, that her father was dead, and that she
was living "in maiden meditation" at Lyme with one of
her guardians, Mr. Andrew Tucker.   In his chance visits
to that place, young Fielding appears to have become
desperately enamoured of her, and to have sadly flut-
tered the Dorset dovecotes by his pertinacious and un-
desirable attentions.   At one time he seems to have
actually meditated the abduction of his "flame," for an
entry in the town archives, discovered by Mr. George
Roberts, sometime Mayor of Lyme, who tells the story,
declares that Andrew Tucker, Esq., went in fear of his
life "owing to the behaviour of Henry Fielding and his
attendant, or man."   Such a state of things (especially
when guardians have sons of their own) is clearly not
to be endured; and Miss Andrew was prudently trans-

ferred to the care of another guardian, Mr. Rhodes of
Modbury, in South Devon, to whose son, a young gentleman of Oxford, she was promptly married. Burke
(*Landed Gentry*, 1858) dates the marriage in 1726, a date
which is practically confirmed by the baptism of a child
at Modbury in April of the following year.[1] Burke
further describes the husband as Mr. Ambrose Rhodes
of Buckland House, Buckland-Tout-Saints. His son, Mr.
Rhodes of Bellair, near Exeter, was gentleman of the
Privy Chamber to George III. ; and one of his descendants possessed a picture which passed for the portrait of
Sophia Western. The tradition of the Tucker family
pointed to Miss Andrew as the original of Fielding's
heroine ; but though such a supposition is intelligible, it
is untenable, since he says distinctly (Book XIII. chap. i.
of *Tom Jones*) that his model was his first wife, whose
likeness he moreover draws very specifically in another
place, by declaring that she resembled Margaret Cecil,
Lady Ranelagh, and, more nearly, "the famous Dutchess
of *Mazarine.*"

With this early escapade is perhaps to be connected
what seems to have been one of Fielding's earliest literary
efforts. This is a modernisation in burlesque octosyllabic
verse of part of Juvenal's sixth satire. In the "Preface"
to the later published *Miscellanies*, it is said to have been
"originally sketched out before he was Twenty," and to
have constituted "all the Revenge taken by an injured
Lover." But it must have been largely revised subsequent
to that date, for it contains references to Mrs. Clive, Mrs.
Woffington, Cibber the younger, and even to Richardson's
Pamela. It has no special merit, although some of the

[1] This has been ascertained from the Modbury parish registers.

couplets have the true Swiftian turn.   If Murphy's statement be correct, that the author "went from Eton to
Leyden," it must have been planned at the latter place,
where, he tells us in the preface to *Don Quixote in England*, he also began that comedy.   Notwithstanding these
literary distractions, he is nevertheless reported to have
studied the civilians "with a remarkable application for
about two years."   At the expiration of this time, remit-
tances from home failing, he was obliged to forego the
lectures of the "learned Vitriarius" (then Professor of
Civil Law at Leyden University), and return to London,
which he did at the beginning of 1728 or the end of
1727.

The fact was that his father, never a rich man,
had married again.   His second wife was a widow
named Eleanor Rasa; and by this time he was fast ac-
quiring a second family.   Under the pressure of his
growing cares, he found himself, however willing, as
unable to maintain his eldest son in London as he had
previously been to discharge his expenses at Leyden.
Nominally, he made him an allowance of two hundred
a year; but this, as Fielding himself explained, "any
body might pay that would."   The consequence was, that
not long after the arrival of the latter in the Metropolis
he had given up all idea of pursuing the law, to which
his mother's legal connections had perhaps first attracted
him, and had determined to adopt the more seductive
occupation of living by his wits.   At this date he was
in the prime of youth.   From the portrait by Hogarth
representing him at a time when he was broken in health
and had lost his teeth, it is difficult to reconstruct his
likeness at twenty.   But we may fairly assume the "high-

arched Roman nose" with which his enemies reproached
him, the dark eyes, the prominent chin, and the humorous
expression; and it is clear that he must have been tall
and vigorous, for he was over six feet when he died, and
had been remarkably strong and active. Add to this
that he inherited a splendid constitution, with an un-
limited capacity for enjoyment, and we have a fair idea
of Henry Fielding at that moment of his career, when
with passions "tremblingly alive all o'er"—as Murphy
says—he stood,

"This way and that dividing the swift mind,"

between the professions of hackney-writer and hackney-
coachman. His natural bias was towards literature, and
his opportunities, if not his inclinations, directed him to
dramatic writing.

It is not necessary to attempt any detailed account
of the state of the stage at this epoch. Nevertheless, if
only to avoid confusion in the future, it will be well to
enumerate the several London theatres in 1728, the
more especially as the list is by no means lengthy.
First and foremost there was the old Opera House in
the Haymarket, built by Vanbrugh, as far back as 1705,
upon the site now occupied by Her Majesty's Theatre.
This was the home of that popular Italian song which so
excited the anger of thorough-going Britons; and here,
at the beginning of 1728, they were performing Handel's
opera of *Siroe*, and delighting the *cognoscenti* by *Dite che
fà*, the echo-air in the same composer's *Tolomeo*. Opposite the Opera House, and, in position, only "a few feet
distant" from the existing Haymarket Theatre, was the
New, or Little Theatre in the Haymarket, which, from

the fact that it had been opened eight years before by
"the French Comedians," was also sometimes styled
the French House. Next comes the no-longer-existent
theatre in Lincoln's Inn Fields, which Christopher Rich
had rebuilt in 1714, and which his son John had made
notorious for pantomimes. Here the *Beggar's Opera*,
precursor of a long line of similar productions, had just
been successfully produced. Finally, most ancient of
them all, there was the Theatre-Royal in Drury Lane,
otherwise the King's Play House, or Old House. The
virtual patentees at this time were the actors Colley
Cibber, Robert Wilks, and Barton Booth. The two former were just playing the *Provok'd Husband*, in which the
famous Mrs. Oldfield (Pope's "Narcissa") had created
a *furore* by her assumption of Lady Townley. These, in
February 1728, were the four principal London theatres.
Goodman's Fields, where Garrick made his *début*, was not
opened until the following year, and Covent Garden
belongs to a still later date.

Fielding's first dramatic essay—or, to speak more
precisely, the first of his dramatic essays that was produced upon the stage—was a five-act comedy entitled
Love in Several Masques. It was played at Drury Lane
in February 1728, succeeding the *Provok'd Husband*. In
his "Preface" the young author refers to the disadvantage under which he laboured in following close upon
that comedy, and also in being "cotemporary with an
Entertainment which engrosses the whole Talk and
Admiration of the Town,"—*i.e.* the *Beggar's Opera*. He
also acknowledges the kindness of Wilks and Cibber
"previous to its Representation," and the fact that he
had thus acquired their suffrages makes it doubtful

whether his stay at Leyden was not really briefer than
is generally supposed, or that he left Eton much earlier.
In either case he must have been in London some months
before *Love in Several Masques* appeared, for a first play
by an untried youth of twenty, however promising, is
not easily brought upon the boards in any era; and from
his own utterances in *Pasquin*, ten years later, it is clear
that it was no easier then than now.   The sentiments
of the Fustian of that piece in the following protest
probably give an accurate picture of the average dramatic
experiences of Henry Fielding :—

"These little things, Mr. *Sneerwell*, will sometimes happen.   Indeed a Poet undergoes a great deal before he comes
to his Third Night ; first with the Muses, who are humorous
Ladies, and must be attended ; for if they take it into their
Head at any time to go abroad and leave you, you will pump
your Brain in vain : Then, Sir, with the Master of a *Play-
house* to get it acted, *whom you generally follow a quarter of a
Year before you know whether he will receive it or no ;* and then
perhaps he tells you it won't do, and returns it you again,
reserving the Subject, and perhaps the Name, which he
brings out in his next *Pantomime ;* but if he should receive
the Play, then you must attend again to get it writ out into
Parts, and Rehears'd.   Well, Sir, at last the Rehearsals begin ;
then, Sir, begins another Scene of Trouble with the Actors,
some of whom dont like their Parts, and all are continually
plaguing you with Alterations : At length, after having waded
thro' all these Difficulties, his [the ?] Play appears on the Stage,
where one Man Hisses out of Resentment to the Author ; a
Second out of Dislike to the House ; a Third out of Dislike to
the Actor ; a Fourth out of Dislike to the Play ; a Fifth for
the Joke sake ; a Sixth to keep all the rest in Company.
Enemies abuse him, Friends give him up, the Play is damn'd,
and the Author goes to the Devil, so ends the Farce."

To which Sneerwell replies, with much promptitude :

" The Tragedy rather, I think, Mr. *Fustian.*"   But whatever may have been its preliminary difficulties, Fielding's
first play was not exposed to so untoward a fate.   It was
well received.   As might be expected in a beginner, and
as indeed the references in the Preface to Wycherley
and Congreve would lead us to expect, it was an obvious
attempt in the manner of those then all-popular writers.
The dialogue is ready and witty.   But the characters have
that obvious defect which Lord Beaconsfield recognised
when he spoke in later life of his own earliest efforts.
"Books written by boys," he says, " which pretend to
give a picture of manners and to deal in knowledge of
human nature must necessarily be founded on affectation."
To this rule the personages of *Love in Several Masques* are
no exception.   They are drawn rather from the stage
than from life, and there is little constructive skill in
the plot.   A certain booby squire, Sir Positive Trap,
seems like a first indication of some of the later successes
in the novels ; but the rest of the *dramatis personæ* are
puppets.   The success of the piece was probably owing
to the acting of Mrs. Oldfield, who took the part of
Lady Matchless, a character closely related to the Lady
Townleys and Lady Betty Modishes, in which she won
her triumphs.   She seems, indeed, to have been unusually interested in this comedy, for she consented to
play in it notwithstanding a " slight Indisposition " contracted " by her violent Fatigue in the Part of Lady
Townly," and she assisted the author with her correc-
tions and advice — perhaps with her influence as an
actress.   Fielding's distinguished kinswoman Lady Mary
Wortley Montagu also read the MS.   Looking to certain
scenes in it, the protestation in the Prologue—

" Nought shall offend the Fair Ones Ears to-day,
Which they might blush to hear, or blush to say "—

has an air of insincerity, although, contrasted with some
of the writer's later productions, *Love in Several Masques*
is comparatively pure. But he might honestly think
that the work which had received the *imprimatur* of a
stage-queen and a lady of quality should fairly be regarded as morally blameless, and it is not necessary to
bring any bulk of evidence to prove that the morality of
1728 differed from the morality of to-day.

To the last-mentioned year is ascribed a poem entitled
the "*Masquerade*. Inscribed to C—t H—d—g—r. By
Lemuel Gulliver, Poet Laureate to the King of Lilliput."
In this Fielding made his satirical contribution to the
attacks on those impure gatherings organised by the
notorious Heidegger, which Hogarth had not long before
stigmatised pictorially in the plate known to collectors as
the "large Masquerade Ticket." As verse this performance
is worthless, and it is not very forcibly on the side of good
manners ; but the ironic dedication has a certain touch
of Fielding's later fashion. Two other poetical pieces,
afterwards included in the *Miscellanies* of 1743, also bear
the date of 1728. One is *A Description of U—n G—*
(alias *New Hog's Norton*) *in Com. Hants*, which Mr.
Keightley has identified with Upton Grey, near Odiham,
in Hampshire. It is a burlesque description of a tumble-
down country-house in which the writer was staying,
and is addressed to Rosalinda. The other is entitled
To Euthalia, from which it must be concluded that, in
1728, Sarah Andrew had found more than one successor.
But in spite of some biographers, and of the apparent
encouragement given to his first comedy, Fielding does

not seem to have followed up dramatic authorship with
equal vigour, or at all events with equal success. His real
connection with the stage does not begin until January
1730, when the *Temple Beau* was produced by Giffard
the actor at the theatre in Goodman's Fields, which had
then just been opened by Thomas Odell ; and it may be
presumed that his incentive was rather want of funds
than desire of fame. *The Temple Beau* certainly shows
an advance upon its predecessor ; but it is an advance in
the same direction, imitation of Congreve ; and although
Geneste ranks it among the best of Fielding's plays, it
is doubtful whether modern criticism would sustain his
verdict. It ran for a short time, and was then withdrawn. The Prologue was the work of James Ralph,
afterwards Fielding's colleague in the *Champion*, and it
thus refers to the prevailing taste. The *Beggar's Opera*
had killed Italian song, but now a new danger had
arisen,—

> " *Humour and Wit, in each politer Age,*
> *Triumphant, rear'd the Trophies of the Stage :*
> *But only Farce, and Shew, will now go down,*
> *And* Harlequin's *the Darling of the Town.*"

As if to confirm his friend's opinion, Fielding's next
piece combined the popular ingredients above referred
to. In March following he produced at the Haymarket,
under the pseudonym of Scriblerus Secundus, *The
Author's Farce*, with a "Puppet Show" called *The
Pleasures of the Town*. In the Puppet Show, Henley,
the Clare-Market Orator, and Samuel Johnson, the
quack author of the popular *Hurlothrumbo*, were smartly
satirised, as also was the fashionable craze for Opera and
Pantomime. But the most enduring part of this odd

medley is the farce which occupies the two first acts, and under thin disguises no doubt depicts much which was within the writer's experience. At all events, Luckless, the author in the play, has more than one of the characteristics which distinguish the traditional portrait of Fielding himself in his early years. He wears a laced coat, is in love, writes plays, and cannot pay his landlady, who declares, with some show of justice, that she "would no more depend on a Benefit-Night of an un-acted Play, than she wou'd on a Benefit-Ticket in an un-drawn Lottery." "Her Floor (she laments) is all spoil'd with Ink—her Windows with Verses, and her Door has been almost beat down with Duns." But the most humorous scenes in the play—scenes really admirable in their ironic delineation of the seamy side of authorship in 1730—are those in which Mr. Bookweight, the publisher—the Curll or Osborne of the period—is shown surrounded by the obedient hacks, who feed at his table on "good Milk-porridge, very often twice a Day," and manufacture the murders, ghost-stories, political pamphlets, and translations from Virgil (out of Dryden) with which he supplies his customers. Here is one of them as good as any :—

" *Bookweight.* So, Mr. *Index*, what News with you?
Index. I have brought my Bill, Sir.
Book. What's here?—for fitting the Motto of *Risum teneatis Amici* to a dozen Pamphlets at Sixpence per each, Six Shillings — For *Omnia vincit Amor, & nos cedamus Amori,* Sixpence—For *Difficile est Satyram non scribere,* Sixpence— Hum! hum! hum! Sum total, for Thirty-six *Latin* Motto's, Eighteen Shillings; ditto *English,* One Shilling and Nine- pence ; ditto *Greek,* Four, Four Shillings. These *Greek* Motto's are excessively dear.

Ind. If you have them cheaper at either of the Universities, I will give you mine for nothing.

Book. You shall have your Money immediately, and pray remember that I must have two *Latin* Seditious Motto's and one *Greek* Moral Motto for Pamphlets by to-morrow Morning. . . .

Ind. Sir, I shall provide them. Be pleas'd to look on that, Sir, and print me Five hundred Proposals, and as many Receipts.

Book. Proposals for printing by Subscription a new Translation of Cicero, *Of the Nature of the Gods and his Tusculan Questions,* by *Jeremy Index,* Esq. ; I am sorry you have undertaken this, for it prevents a Design of mine.

Ind. Indeed, Sir, it does not, for you see all of the Book that I ever intend to publish. It is only a handsome Way of asking one's Friends for a Guinea.

Book. Then you have not translated a Word of it, perhaps.

Ind. Not a single Syllable.

Book. Well, you shall have your Proposals forthwith ; but I desire you wou'd be a little more reasonable in your Bills for the future, or I shall deal with you no longer ; for I have a certain Fellow of a College, who offers to furnish me with Second-hand Motto's out of the *Spectator* for Two-pence each.

Ind. Sir, I only desire to live by my Goods, and I hope you will be pleas'd to allow some difference between a neat fresh Piece, piping hot out of the Classicks, and old thread-bare worn-out Stuff that has past thro' ev'ry Pedant's Mouth. . . ."

The latter part of this amusing dialogue, referring to Mr. Index's translation from Cicero, was added in an amended version of the *Author's Farce,* which appeared some years later, and in which Fielding depicts the portrait of another all-powerful personage in the literary life,—the actor-manager. This, however, will be more conveniently treated under its proper date, and it is only necessary to say here that the slight sketches of Marplay and

Sparkish given in the first edition, were presumably intended for Cibber and Wilks, with whom, notwithstanding the "civil and kind Behaviour" for which he had thanked them in the "Preface" to *Love in Several Masques*, the young dramatist was now, it seems, at war. In the introduction to the *Miscellanies*, he refers to "a slight Pique" with Wilks; and it is not impossible that the key to the difference may be found in the following passage :—

> "*Sparkish.* What dost think of the Play ?
> *Marplay.* It may be a very good one, for ought I know ; *but I know the Author has no Interest.*
> *Spark.* Give me Interest, and rat the Play.
> *Mar.* Rather rat the Play which has no Interest. Interest sways as much in the Theatre as at Court.—And you know it is not always the Companion of Merit in either."

The handsome student from Leyden — the potential Congreve who wrote *Love in Several Masques*, and had Lady Mary Wortley Montagu for patroness, might fairly be supposed to have expectations which warranted the civilities of Messrs. Wilks and Cibber ; but the "Luckless" of two years later had probably convinced them that his dramatic performances did not involve their *sine qua non* of success. Under these circumstances nothing perhaps could be more natural than that they should play their parts in his little satire.

We have dwelt at some length upon the *Author's Farce*, because it is the first of Fielding's plays in which, leaving the "wit-traps" of Wycherley and Congreve, he deals with the direct censure of contemporary folly, and because, apart from translation and adaptation, it is in this field that his most brilliant theatrical successes were

won. For the next few years he continued to produce
comedies and farces with great rapidity, both under his
own name, and under the pseudonym of Scriblerus Secundus. Most of these show manifest signs of haste, and
some are recklessly immodest. We shall confine our-
selves to one or two of the best, and do little more than
enumerate the others. Of these latter, the *Coffee-House
Politician ; or, The Justice caught in his own Trap*, 1730,
succeeded the *Author's Farce.* The leading idea, that of
a tradesman who neglects his shop for " foreign affairs,"
appears to be derived from Addison's excellent character-
sketch in the *Tatler* of the " Political Upholsterer." This
is the more likely, in that Arne the musician, whose
father is generally supposed to have been Addison's
original, was Fielding's contemporary at Eton. Justice
Squeezum, another character contained in this play, is
a kind of first draft of the later Justice Thrasher in
Amelia. The representation of the trading justice on
the stage, however, was by no means new, since Justice
Quorum in Coffey's *Beggar's Wedding* (with whom, as will
appear presently, Fielding's name has been erroneously
associated) exhibits similar characteristics. Omitting for
the moment the burlesque of *Tom Thumb,* the *Coffee-House
Politician* was followed by the *Letter Writers ; or, A new
Way to Keep a Wife at Home,* 1731, a brisk little farce, with
one vigorously drawn character, that of Jack Commons, a
young university rake ; the *Grub-Street Opera,* 1731 ; the
farce of the *Lottery,* 1731, in which the famous Mrs. Clive,
then Miss Raftor, appeared ; the *Modern Husband,* 1732 ;
the *Covent Garden Tragedy,* 1732, a broad and rather
riotous burlesque of Ambrose Philips' *Distrest Mother ;*
and the *Debauchees ; or, The Jesuit Caught,* 1732—which

was based upon the then debated story of Father Girard and Catherine Cadière.

Neither of the two last-named pieces is worthy of the author, and their strongest condemnation in our day is that they were condemned in their own for their un-bridled license, the *Grub Street Journal* going so far as to say that they had "met with the universal detestation of the Town." The *Modern Husband*, which turns on that most loathsome of all commercial pursuits, the traffic of a husband in his wife's dishonour, appears, oddly enough, to have been regarded by its author with espe-cial complacency. Its prologue lays stress upon the moral purpose ; it was dedicated to Sir Robert Walpole ; and from a couple of letters printed in Lady Mary Wort-ley Montagu's *Correspondence*, it is clear that it had been submitted to her perusal. It had, however, no great success upon the stage, and the chief thing worth re-membering about it is that it afforded his last character to Wilks, who played the part of Bellamant. That "slight Pique," of which mention has been made, was no doubt by this time a thing of the past.

But if most of the works in the foregoing list can hardly be regarded as creditable to Fielding's artistic or moral sense, one of them at least deserves to be excepted, and that is the burlesque of *Tom Thumb*. This was first brought out in 1730 at the little theatre in the Hay-market, where it met with a favourable reception. In the following year it was enlarged to three acts (in the first version there had been but two), and reproduced at the same theatre as the *Tragedy of Tragedies; or, The Life and Death of Tom Thumb the Great*, "with the Anno-tations of H. Scriblerus Secundus." It is certainly one

of the best burlesques ever written.   As Baker observes
in his *Biographia Dramatica*, it may fairly be ranked as
a sequel to Buckingham's *Rehearsal*, since it includes the
absurdities of nearly all the writers of tragedies from
the period when that piece stops to 1730.   Among the
authors satirised are Nat. Lee, Thomson (whose famous

> " O Sophonisba, Sophonisba, O !"

is parodied by

> " O Huncamunca, Huncamunca, O !"),

Banks's *Earl of Essex*, a favourite play at Bartholomew
Fair, the *Busiris* of Young, and the *Aurengzebe* of Dryden, etc.   The annotations, which abound in transparent
references to Dr. B[*entle*]y, Mr. T[*heobal*]d, Mr. D[*enni*]s,
are excellent imitations of contemporary pedantry.   One
example, elicited in Act 1 by a reference to "giants,"
must stand for many :—

"That learned Historian Mr. S———n in the third Number of his Criticism on our Author, takes great Pains to
explode this Passage.   It is, says he, difficult to guess what
Giants are here meant, unless the Giant *Despair* in the *Pil-
grim's Progress*, or the giant *Greatness* in the *Royal Villain;*
for I have heard of no other sort of Giants in the Reign
of King *Arthur*.   *Petrus Burmanus* makes three *Tom Thumbs*,
one whereof he supposes to have been the same Person whom
the *Greeks* called *Hercules*, and that by these Giants are to be
understood the *Centaurs* slain by that Heroe.   Another *Tom
Thumb* he contends to have been no other than the *Hermes
Trismegistus* of the Antients.   The third *Tom Thumb* he places
under the Reign of King *Arthur;* to which third *Tom Thumb*,
says he, the Actions of the other two were attributed.   Now,
tho' I know that this Opinion is supported by an Assertion
of *Justus Lipsius, Thomam illum Thumbum non alium quam*

Herculem fuisse satis constat; yet shall I venture to oppose one Line of Mr. *Midwinter*, against them all,

> *In* Arthurs' *Court* Tom Thumb *did live.*

"But then, says Dr. *B——y*, if we place *Tom Thumb* in the Court of King *Arthur*, it will be proper to place that Court out of *Britain*, where no Giants were ever heard of. *Spencer*, in his *Fairy Queen*, is of another Opinion, where describing *Albion*, he says,

> Far within, a salvage Nation dwelt
> Of hideous Giants.

And in the same canto :

> *Then* Elfar, *with two Brethren Giants had*
> *The one of which had two Heads,—*
> > *The other three.*

Risum teneatis, Amici."

Of the play itself it is difficult to give an idea by extract, as nearly every line travesties some tragic passage once familiar to play-goers, and now utterly forgotten. But the following lines from one of the speeches of Lord Grizzle—a part admirably acted by Liston in later years[1]—are a fair specimen of its ludicrous use (or rather abuse) of simile:—

> "Yet think not long, I will my Rival bear,
> Or unreveng'd the slighted Willow wear ;
> The gloomy, brooding Tempest now confin'd,
> Within the hollow Caverns of my Mind,
> In dreadful Whirl, shall rowl along the Coasts,
> Shall thin the Land of all the Men it boasts,
> And cram up ev'ry Chink of Hell with Ghosts.
> So have I seen, in some dark Winter's Day,
> A sudden Storm rush down the Sky's High-Way,
> Sweep thro' the Streets with terrible ding-dong,
> Gush thro' the Spouts, and wash whole Crowds along.

---

[1] Compare Hazlitt, *On the Comic Writers of the Last Century.*

The crowded Shops, the thronging Vermin skreen,
Together cram the Dirty and the Clean,
And not one Shoe-Boy in the Street is seen."

In the modern version of Kane O'Hara, to which
songs were added, the *Tragedy of Tragedies* still keeps, or
kept the stage. But its crowning glory is its traditional
connection with Swift, who told Mrs. Pilkington that he
"had not laugh'd above twice" in his life, once at the
tricks of a merry-andrew, and again when (in Fielding's
burlesque) Tom Thumb killed the ghost. This is an
incident of the earlier versions, omitted in deference to
the critics, for which the reader will seek vainly in the
play as now printed; and even then he will discover that
Mrs. Pilkington's memory served her imperfectly, since
it is not Tom Thumb who kills the ghost, but the ghost
of Tom Thumb which is killed by his jealous rival,
Lord Grizzle. A trifling inaccuracy of this sort, however, is rather in favour of the truth of the story than
against it, for a pure fiction would in all probability have
been more precise. Another point of interest in connection with this burlesque is the frontispiece which Hogarth
supplied to the edition of 1731. It has no special value
as a design, but it constitutes the earliest reference to
that friendship with the painter, of which so many traces
are to be found in Fielding's works.

Hitherto Fielding had succeeded best in burlesque.
But, in 1732, the same year in which he produced the
Modern Husband, the *Debauchees,* and the *Covent Garden
Tragedy,* he made an adaptation of Molière's *Médecin
malgré lui,* which had already been imitated in English
by Mrs. Centlivre and others. This little piece, to which
he gave the title of the *Mock-Doctor; or, The Dumb Lady*

cur'd, was well received. The French original was rendered with tolerable closeness; but here and there
Fielding has introduced little touches of his own, as,
for instance, where Gregory (Sganarelle) tells his wife
Dorcas (Martine), whom he has just been beating, that
as they are but one, whenever he beats her he beats half
of himself. To this she replies by requesting that for
the future he will beat the other half. An entire scene
(the thirteenth) was also added at the desire of Miss
Raftor, who played Dorcas, and thought her part too
short. This is apparently intended as a burlesque of
the notorious quack Misaubin, to whom the *Mock-Doctor*
was ironically dedicated. He was the proprietor of a
famous pill, and was introduced by Hogarth into the
Harlot's Progress. Gregory was played by Theophilus
Cibber, and the preface contains a complimentary reference to his acting, and the expected retirement of his
father from the stage. Neither Geneste nor Lawrence
gives the date when the piece was first produced, but if
the "April" on the dubious author's benefit ticket attributed to Hogarth be correct, it must have been in the
first months of 1732.

The cordial reception of the *Mock-Doctor* seems to have
encouraged Fielding to make further levies upon Molière,
and he speaks of his hope to do so in the "Preface." As
a matter of fact, he produced a version of *L'Avare* at
Drury Lane in the following year, which entirely out-
shone the older versions of Shadwell and Ozell, and
gained from Voltaire the praise of having added to the
original "*quelques beautés de dialogue particulières à sâ*
(Fielding's) *nation.*" Lovegold, its leading *rôle,* became
a stock part. It was well played by its first actor Griffin,

and was a favourite exercise with Macklin, Shuter, and (in our own days) Phelps.

In February 1733, when the *Miser* was first acted, Fielding was five and twenty. His means at this time were, in all probability, exceedingly uncertain. The small proportion of money due to him at his mother's death had doubtless been long since exhausted, and he must have been almost wholly dependent upon the precarious profits of his pen. That he was assisted by rich and noble friends to any material extent appears, in spite of Murphy, to be unlikely. At all events, an occasional dedication to the Duke of Richmond or the Earl of Chesterfield cannot be regarded as proof positive. Lyttelton, who certainly befriended him in later life, was for a great part of this period absent on the Grand Tour, and Ralph Allen had not yet come forward. In default of the always deferred allowance, his father's house at Salisbury (?) was no doubt open to him ; and it is plain, from indications in his minor poems, that he occasionally escaped into the country. But in London he lived for the most part, and probably not very worshipfully. What, even now, would be the life of a young man of Fielding's age, fond of pleasure, careless of the future, very liberally equipped with high spirits, and straightway exposed to the perilous seductions of the stage ? Fielding had the defects of his qualities, and was no better than the rest of those about him. He was manly, and frank, and generous; but these characteristics could scarcely protect him from the terrors of the tip-staff, and the sequels of "t'other bottle." Indeed, he very honestly and unfeignedly confesses to the lapses of his youth in the *Journey from this World to the Next*, adding that he pretended "to very little Virtue more than general Philanthropy and private Friendship." It is therefore but reasonable to infer that his daily life must have been more than usually characterised by the vicissitudes of the eighteenth-century prodigal,—alternations from the "Rose" to a Clare-Market ordinary, from gold-lace to fustian, from champagne to "British Burgundy." In a rhymed petition to Walpole, dated 1730, he makes pleasant mirth of what no doubt was sometimes sober truth—his debts, his duns, and his dinnerless condition. He (the verses tell us)

> "—— from his Garret can look down
> On the whole Street of *Arlington.*" [1]

Again—

> "The Family that dines the latest
> Is in our Street esteem'd the greatest ;
> But latest Hours must surely fall
> Before him who ne'er dines at all ;"

and

> "This too doth in my Favour speak,
> Your Levée is but twice a Week ;
> From mine I can exclude but one Day,
> My Door is quiet on a *Sunday.*"

When he can admit so much even jestingly of himself, it is but legitimate to presume that there is no great exaggeration in the portrait of him in 1735, by the anonymous satirist of *Seasonable Reproof :*—

> "*F*—— *g*, who *yesterday* appear'd so rough,
> Clad in *coarse Frize*, and plaister'd down with *Snuff*,
> See how his *Instant* gaudy Trappings shine ;
> What *Play-house* Bard was ever seen so fine !
> But this, not from his *Humour* flows, you'll say,

---

[1] Where Sir Robert lived.

But mere *Necessity ;*—for last Night lay
In *Pawn*, the *Velvet* which he wears to Day."

His work bears traces of the inequalities and irregu-
larities of his mode of living. Although in certain cases
(*e.g.* the revised edition of *Tom Thumb*) the artist and
scholar seems to have spasmodically asserted himself,
the majority of his plays were hasty and ill-considered
performances, most of which (as Lady Mary said) he
would have thrown into the fire " if meat could have been
got without money, and money without scribbling."
" When he had contracted to bring on a play, or a farce,"
says Murphy, " it is well known, by many of his friends
now living, that he would go home rather late from a
tavern, and would, the next morning, deliver a scene to the
players, written upon the papers which had wrapped the
tobacco, in which he so much delighted." It is not easy
to conceive, unless Fielding's capacities as a smoker were
phenomenal, that any large contribution to dramatic
literature could have been made upon the wrappings of
Virginia or Freeman's Best; but that his reputation
for careless production was established among his contemporaries is manifest from the following passage in
a burlesque *Author's Will* published in the *Universal
Spectator* of Oldys :—

" *Item*, I give and bequeath to my very *negligent* Friend
Henry Drama, Esq., all my INDUSTRY. And whereas the
World may think this an unnecessary Legacy, forasmuch as
the said *Henry Drama*, Esq., brings on the Stage *four Pieces*
every Season ; yet as such Pieces are always wrote with un-
common *Rapidity*, and during such fatal Intervals only as
the *Stocks* have been on the *Fall*, this Legacy will be of use
to him to revise and correct his Works. Furthermore, for
fear the said *Henry Drama* should make an ill Use of the

said *Industry*, and expend it all on a *Ballad Farce*, it's my Will the said Legacy should be paid him by equal Portions, and as his Necessities may require."

There can be little doubt that the above quotation, which is reprinted in the *Gentleman's* for July 1734, and seems to have hitherto escaped inquiry, refers to none other than the "very negligent" Author of the *Modern Husband* and the *Old Debauchees*—in other words, to Henry Fielding.

CHAPTER II.

THE very subordinate part in the *Miser* of "Furnish, an Upholsterer," was taken by a third-rate actor, whose surname has been productive of no little misconception among Henry Fielding's biographers. This was Timothy Fielding, sometime member of the Haymarket and Drury Lane companies, and proprietor, for several successive years, of a booth at Bartholomew, Southwark, and other fairs. In the absence of any Christian name, Mr. Lawrence seems to have rather rashly concluded that the Fielding mentioned by Geneste as having a booth at Bartholomew Fair in 1733 with Hippisley (the original Peachum of the *Beggar's Opera*), was Fielding the dramatist; and the mistake thus originated at once began that prosperous course which usually awaits any slip of the kind. It misled one notoriously careful inquirer, who, in his interesting chronicles of Bartholomew Fair, minutely investigated the actor's history, giving precise details of his doings at "Bartlemy" from 1728 to 1736; but, although the theory involved obvious inconsistencies, apparently without any suspicion that the proprietor of the booth which stood, season after season, in the yard of the George Inn at Smithfield, was an entirely different person from his greater namesake. The late Dr. Rimbault carried the story farther still, and attempted to show, in *Notes and Queries* for May 1859, that Henry Fielding had a booth at Tottenham Court in 1738, "subsequent to his admission into the Middle Temple;" and he also promised to supply additional particulars to the effect that even 1738 was not the "*last* year of Fielding's career as a booth-proprietor." At this stage (probably for good reasons) inquiry seems to have slumbered, although, with the fatal vitality of error, the statement continued (and still continues) to be repeated in various quarters. In 1875, however, Mr. Frederick Latreille published a short article in *Notes and Queries*, proving conclusively, by extracts from contemporary newspapers and other sources, that the Timothy Fielding above referred to was the real Fielding of the fairs; that he became landlord of the Buffalo Tavern "at the corner of Bloomsbury Square" in 1733; and that he died in August 1738, his christian name, so often suppressed, being dûly recorded in the register of the neighbouring church of St. George's, where he was buried. The admirers of our great novelist owe Mr. Latreille a debt of gratitude for this opportune discovery. It is true that a certain element of Bohemian picturesqueness is lost to Henry Fielding's life, already not very rich in recorded incident; and it would certainly have been curious if he, who ended his days in trying to dignify the judicial office, should have begun life by acting the part of a "trading justice," namely that of Quorum in Coffey's *Beggar's Wedding*, which Timothy Fielding had played at Drury Lane. But, on the whole, it is satisfactory to know that his early experiences did not, of necessity, include those of a strolling player. Some obscure and temporary connection with Bartholomew Fair he may have had, as Smollett, in the scurrilous pamphlet issued in 1742, makes him say that he blew a trumpet there in quality of herald to a collection of wild beasts; but this is probably no more than an earlier and uglier form of the apparition laid by Mr. Latreille. The only positive evidence of any connection between Henry Fielding and the Smithfield carnival is, that Theophilus Cibber's company played the *Miser* at their booth in August 1733.

With the exception of the *Miser* and an afterpiece, never printed, entitled *Deborah; or, A Wife for you all*, which was acted for Miss Raftor's benefit in April 1733, nothing important was brought upon the stage by Fielding until January of the following year, when he produced the *Intriguing Chambermaid*, and a revised version of the *Author's Farce*. By a succession of changes, which it is impossible here to describe in detail, consider-able alterations had taken place in the management of Drury Lane. In the first place, Wilks was dead, and his share in the Patent was represented by his widow. Booth also was dead, and Mrs. Booth had sold her share to Giffard of Goodman's Fields, while the elder Cibber had retired. At the beginning of the season of 1733-34 the leading patentee was an amateur called Highmore, who had purchased Cibber's share. He had also purchased part of Booth's share before his death in May 1733. The only other shareholder of importance was Mrs. Wilks. Shortly after the opening of the theatre in September, the greater part of the Drury Lane Company, led by the younger Cibber, revolted

from Highmore and Mrs. Wilks, and set up for themselves. Matters were farther complicated by the fact
that John Rich had not long opened a new theatre in
Covent Garden, which constituted a fresh attraction;
and that what Fielding called the "wanton affected
Fondness for foreign Musick," was making the Italian
opera a dangerous rival—the more so as it was patronised
by the nobility. Without actors, the patentees were in
serious case. Miss Raftor, who about this time became
Mrs. Clive, appears, however, to have remained faithful
to them, as also did Henry Fielding. The lively little
comedy of the *Intriguing Chambermaid* was adapted from
Regnard especially for her; and in its published form
was preceded by an epistle in which the dramatist dwells
upon the "Factions and Divisions among the Players,"
and compliments her upon her compassionate adherence
to Mr. Highmore and Mrs. Wilks in their time of need.
The epistle is also valuable for its warm and generous
testimony to the private character of this accomplished
actress, whose part in real life, says Fielding, was that of
"the best Wife, the best Daughter, the best Sister, and
the best Friend." The words are more than mere compliment; they appear to have been true. Madcap and
humourist as she was, no breath of slander seems ever
to have tarnished the reputation of Kitty Clive, whom
Johnson—a fine judge, when his prejudices were not
actively aroused—called in addition "the best player
that he ever saw."

The *Intriguing Chambermaid* was produced on the 15th
of January 1734. Lettice, from whom the piece was
named, was well personated by Mrs. Clive, and Colonel
Bluff by Macklin, the only actor of any promise that

Highmore had been able to secure. With the new comedy the *Author's Farce* was revived. It would be unnecessary to refer to this again, but for the additions that were made to it. These consisted chiefly in the substitution of Marplay Junior for Sparkish, the actor-manager of the first version. The death of Wilks may have been a reason for this alteration; but a stronger was no doubt the desire to throw ridicule upon Theophilus Cibber, whose behaviour in deserting Drury Lane immediately after his father had sold his share to Highmore had not passed without censure, nor had his father's action escaped sarcastic comment. Theophilus Cibber— whose best part was Beaumont and Fletcher's Copper Captain, and who carried the impersonation into private life—had played in several of Fielding's pieces; but Fielding had linked his fortunes to those of the patentees, and was consequently against the players in this quarrel. The following scene was accordingly added to the farce for the exclusive benefit of "Young Marplay":—

"*Marplay junior.* Mr. *Luckless*, I kiss your Hands—Sir, I am your most obedient humble Servant; you see, Mr. *Luckless*, what Power you have over me. I attend your Commands, tho' several Persons of Quality have staid at Court for me above this Hour.

Luckless. I am obliged to you—I have a Tragedy for your House, Mr. *Marplay.*

Mar. jun. Ha! if you will send it me, I will give you my Opinion of it; and if I can make any Alterations in it that will be for its Advantage, I will do it freely.

Witmore. Alterations, Sir?

Mar. jun. Yes, Sir, Alterations—I will maintain it, let a Play be never so good, without Alteration it will do nothing.

Wit. Very odd indeed.

Mar. jun. Did you ever write, Sir ?

Wit. No, Sir, I thank Heav'n.

Mar. jun. Oh ! your humble Servant—your very humble Servant, Sir. When you write yourself you will find the Necessity of Alterations. Why, Sir, wou'd you guess that I had alter'd *Shakespear ?*

Wit. Yes, faith, Sir, no one sooner.

Mar. jun. Alack-a-day ! Was you to see the Plays when they are brought to us—a Parcel of crude, undigested Stuff. We are the Persons, Sir, who lick them into Form, that mould them into Shape — The Poet make the Play indeed ! The Colour-man might be as well said to make the Picture, or the Weaver the Coat : My Father and I, Sir, are a Couple of poetical Tailors ; when a Play is brought us, we consider it as a Tailor does his Coat, we cut it, Sir, we cut it : And let me tell you, we have the exact Measure of the Town, we know how to fit their Taste. The Poets, between you and me, are a Pack of ignorant——

Wit. Hold, hold, sir. This is not quite so civil to Mr. *Luckless :* Besides, as I take it, you have done the Town the Honour of writing yourself.

Mar. jun. Sir, you are a Man of Sense ; and express yourself well. I did, as you say, once make a small Sally into *Parnassus*, took a sort of flying Leap over *Helicon :* But if ever they catch me there again—Sir, the Town have a Prejudice to my Family ; for if any Play cou'd have made them ashamed to damn it, mine must. It was all over Plot. It wou'd have made half a dozen Novels : Nor was it cram'd with a pack of Wit-traps, like *Congreve* and *Wycherly*, where every one knows when the Joke was coming. I defy the sharpest Critick of 'em all to know when any Jokes of mine were coming. The Dialogue was plain, easy, and natural, and not one single Joke in it from the Beginning to the End : Besides, Sir, there was one Scene of tender melancholy Conversation, enough to have melted a Heart of Stone ; and yet they damn'd it : And they damn'd themselves ; for they shall have no more of mine.

Wit. Take pity on the Town, Sir.

Mar. jun. I ! No, Sir, no. I'll write no more. No more ; unless I am forc'd to it.

Luckless. That's no easy thing, *Marplay.*
Mar. jun. Yes, Sir.   Odes, Odes, a Man may be oblig'd to
write those you know."

These concluding lines plainly refer to the elder
Cibber's appointment as Laureate in 1730, and to those
"annual Birth-day Strains," with which he so long delighted the irreverent; while the alteration of Shakespeare and the cobbling of plays generally, satirised
again in a later scene, are strictly in accordance with
contemporary accounts of the manners and customs of
the two dictators of Drury Lane.   The piece indicated
by Marplay Junior was probably Theophilus Cibber's
Lover, which had been produced in January 1731 with
very moderate success.

After the *Intriguing Chambermaid* and the revived
Author's Farce, Fielding seems to have made farther
exertions for "the distressed Actors in Drury Lane."
He had always been an admirer of Cervantes, frequent
references to whose master-work are to be found scattered
through his plays; and he now busied himself with com-
pleting and expanding the loose scenes of the comedy of
Don Quixote in England, which (as before stated) he
had sketched at Leyden for his own diversion.   He
had already thought of bringing it upon the stage,
but had been dissuaded from doing so by Cibber and
Booth, who regarded it as wanting in novelty.   Now,
however, he strengthened it by the addition of some
election scenes, in which—he tells Lord Chesterfield
in the dedication—he designed to give a lively representation of "the Calamities brought on a Country
by general Corruption;" and it was duly rehearsed.
But unexpected delays took place in its production;

the revolted players returned to Drury Lane; and,
lest the actors' benefits should further retard its appearance by postponing it until the winter season,
Fielding transferred it to the Haymarket, where, according to Geneste, it was acted in April 1734. As a play,
Don Quixote in England has few stage qualities and no
plot to speak of. But the Don with his whimsies, and
Sancho with his appetite and string of proverbs, are conceived in something of the spirit of Cervantes. Squire
Badger, too, a rudimentary Squire Western, well represented by Macklin, is vigorously drawn; and the song
of his huntsman Scut, beginning with the fine line "The
dusky Night rides down the Sky," has a verse that
recalls a practice of which Addison accuses Sir Roger
de Coverley :—

> " *A brushing Fox in yonder Wood,*
>   *Secure to find we seek;*
> *For why, I carry'd sound and good,*
> *A Cartload there last Week.*
>   And a Hunting we will go."

The election scenes, though but slightly attached to
the main story, are keenly satirical, and considering that
Hogarth's famous series of kindred prints belongs to a
much later date, must certainly have been novel, as may
be gathered from the following little colloquy between
Mr. Mayor and Messrs. Guzzle and Retail :—

" *Mayor (to Retail)*. . . . I like an Opposition, because
otherwise a Man may be oblig'd to vote against his Party ;
therefore when we invite a Gentleman to stand, we invite
him to spend his Money for the Honour of his Party ; and
when both Parties have spent as much as they are able, every
honest Man will vote according to his Conscience.

Guz. Mr. Mayor talks like a Man of Sense and Honour,
and it does me good to hear him.

May. Ay, ay, Mr. *Guzzle*, I never gave a Vote contrary
to my Conscience. I have very earnestly recommended the
Country-Interest to all my Brethren : But before that, I
recommended the Town-Interest, that is, the interest of this
Corporation ; and first of all I recommended to every particular Man to take a particular Care of himself. And it is
with a certain way of Reasoning, That he who serves me
best, will serve the Town best ; and he that serves the Town
best, will serve the Country best."

In the January and February of 1735 Fielding produced two more pieces at Drury Lane, a farce and a five-
act comedy. The farce—a lively trifle enough—was
An Old Man taught Wisdom, a title subsequently changed
to the *Virgin Unmasked*. It was obviously written to
display the talents of Mrs. Clive, who played in it her
favourite character of a hoyden, and, after "interview-
ing" a number of suitors chosen by her father, finally
ran away with Thomas the footman—a course in those
days not without its parallel in high life, above stairs as
well as below. It appears to have succeeded, though
Bookish, one of the characters, was entirely withdrawn
in deference to some disapprobation on the part of
the audience; while the part of Wormwood, a lawyer,
which is found in the latest editions, is said to have been
"omitted in representation." The comedy, entitled *The
Universal Gallant; or, The different Husbands*, was scarcely
so fortunate. Notwithstanding that Quin, who, after an
absence of many years, had returned to Drury Lane,
played a leading part, and that Theophilus Cibber in the
hero, Captain Smart, seems to have been fitted with a
character exactly suited to his talents and idiosyncrasy,

the play ran no more than three nights.   Till the third
act was almost over, " the *Audience,*" says the *Prompter* (as
quoted by "Sylvanus Urban "), "sat quiet, in hopes it
would mend, till finding it grew *worse* and *worse,* they lost
all Patience, and not an *Expression* or *Sentiment* afterwards
pass'd without its deserved *Censure.*"   Perhaps it is not
to be wondered at that the author—"the prolifick *Mr.
Fielding,*" as the *Prompter* calls him, attributed its condemnation to causes other than its lack of interest.   In
his *Advertisement* he openly complains of the "cruel
Usage" his "poor Play " had met with, and of the bar-
barity of the young men about town who made "a Jest
of damning Plays "—a pastime which, whether it prevailed in this case or not, no doubt existed, as Sarah
Fielding afterwards refers to it in *David Simple.*   If an
author—he goes on to say—"be so unfortunate [*as*] to
depend on the success of his Labours for his Bread, he must
be an inhuman Creature indeed, who would out of sport
and wantonness prevent a Man from getting a Livelihood
in an honest and inoffensive Way, and make a jest of
starving him and his Family."   The plea is a good one
if the play is good; but if not, it is worthless.   In this
respect the public are like the French Cardinal in the
story ; and when the famished writer's work fails to
entertain them, they are fully justified in doubting his
raison d'être.   There is no reason for supposing that the
Universal Gallant deserved a better fate than it met with.

Judging from the time which elapsed between the
production of this play and that of *Pasquin* (Fielding's
next theatrical venture), it has been conjectured that the
interval was occupied by his marriage, and brief experience as a Dorsetshire country gentleman.   The exact

date of his marriage is not known, though it is generally
assumed to have taken place in the beginning of 1735.
But it may well have been earlier, for it will be observed
that in the above quotation from the Preface to the
Universal Gallant, which is dated from "Buckingham
Street, Feb. 12," he indirectly speaks of "his family."
This, it is true, may be no more than the pious fraud of
a bachelor ; but if it be taken literally, we must conclude
that his marriage was already so far a thing of the past
that he was already a father.   This supposition would
account for the absence of any record of the birth of a
child during his forthcoming residence at East Stour,
by the explanation that it had already happened in
London ; and it is not impossible that the entry of the
marriage, too, may be hidden away in some obscure
Metropolitan parish register, since those of Salisbury have
been fruitlessly searched.   At this distance of time, however, speculation is fruitless ; and, in default of more
definite information, the "spring of 1735," which Keightley gives, must be accepted as the probable date of the
marriage.

Concerning the lady, the particulars are more precise.
She was a Miss Charlotte Cradock, one of three sisters
living upon their own means at Salisbury, or—as it was
then styled—New Sarum.   Mr. Keightley's personal
inquiries, *circa* 1858, elicited the information that the
family, now extinct, was highly respectable, but not of
New Sarum's best society.   Richardson, in one of his malevolent outbursts, asserted that the sisters were illegitimate ; but, says the writer above referred to, "of this
circumstance we have no other proof, and I am able to
add that the tradition of Salisbury knows nothing of it."

They were, however, celebrated for their personal attractions; and if the picture given in chap. ii. book iv. of *Tom Jones* accurately represents the first Mrs. Fielding, she must have been a most charming brunette. Something of the stereotyped characteristics of a novelist's heroine obviously enter into the description; but the luxuriant black hair, which, cut "to comply with the modern Fashion," "curled so gracefully in her Neck," the lustrous eyes, the dimple in the right cheek, the chin rather full than small, and the complexion having "more of the Lilly than of the Rose," but flushing with exercise or modesty, are, doubtless, accurately set down. In speaking of the nose as "exactly regular," Fielding appears to have deviated slightly from the truth; for we learn from Lady Louisa Stuart that, in this respect, Miss Cradock's appearance had "suffered a little" from an accident mentioned in book ii. of *Amelia*, the overturning of a chaise. Whether she also possessed the mental qualities and accomplishments which fell to the lot of Sophia Western, we have no means of determining; but Lady Stuart is again our authority for saying that she was as amiable as she was handsome.

From the love-poems in the first volume of the *Miscellanies* of 1743—poems which their author declares to have been "Productions of the Heart rather than of the Head "—it is clear that Fielding had been attached to his future wife for several years previous to 1735. One of them, *Advice to the Nymphs of New S——m*, celebrates the charms of Celia — the poetical equivalent for Charlotte—as early as 1730; another, containing a reference to the player Anthony Boheme, who died in 1731, was probably written at the same time; while a

third, in which, upon the special intervention of Jove
himself, the prize of beauty is decreed by Venus to the
Salisbury sisters, may be of an earlier date than any.
The year 1730 was the year of his third piece, the
Author's Farce, and he must therefore have been paying
his addresses to Miss Cradock not very long after his
arrival in London.   This is a fact to be borne in mind.
So early an attachment to a good and beautiful girl,
living no farther off than Salisbury, where his own father
probably resided, is scarcely consistent with the reckless
dissipation which has been laid to his charge, although,
on his own showing, he was by no means faultless.   But
it is a part of natures like his to exaggerate their errors
in the moment of repentance ; and it may well be that
Henry Fielding, too, was not so black as he painted himself.   Of his love-verses he says—" this Branch of Writing is what I very little pretend to ;" and it would be
misleading to rate them highly, for, unlike his literary
descendant, Mr. Thackeray, he never attained to any
special quality of note.   But some of his octosyllabics,
if they cannot be called equal to Prior's, fall little below
Swift's.   " I hate "—cries he in one of the pieces,

> " I hate the Town, and all its Ways ;
> Ridotto's, Opera's, and Plays ;
> The Ball, the Ring, the Mall, the Court ;
> Wherever the Beau-Monde resort . . .
> All Coffee-Houses, and their Praters ;
> All Courts of Justice, and Debaters ;
> All Taverns, and the Sots within 'em ;
> All Bubbles, and the Rogues that skin 'em,"

—and so forth, the natural anti-climax being that he
loves nothing but his " Charmer " at Salisbury.   In an-

other, which is headed *To Celia.—Occasioned by her appre-*
hending her House would be broke open, and having an old
Fellow to guard it, who sat up all Night, with a Gun without
any Ammunition, and from which it has been concluded
that the Miss Cradocks were their own landlords, Venus
chides Cupid for neglecting to guard her favourite :—

> " ' Come tell me, Urchin, tell no lies ;
>   Where was you hid, in *Vince's* eyes ?
>   Did you fair *Bennet's* Breast importune ?
>   (I know you dearly love a Fortune.) '
>   Poor *Cupid* now began to whine ;
>   ' Mamma, it was no Fault of mine.
>   I in a Dimple lay *perdue*,
>   That little Guard-Room chose by you.
>   A hundred Loves (all arm'd) did grace
>   The Beauties of her Neck and Face ;
>   Thence, by a Sigh I dispossest,
>   Was blown to *Harry Fielding's* Breast ;
>   Where I was forc'd all Night to stay,
>   Because I could not find my Way.
>   But did Mamma know there what Work
>   I've made, how acted like a Turk;
>   What Pains, what Torment he endures,
>   Which no Physician ever cures,
>   She would forgive.'   The Goddess smil'd,
>   And gently chuck'd her wicked Child,
>   Bid him go back, and take more Care,
>   And give her Service to the Fair."

Swift, in his *Rhapsody on Poetry*, 1733, coupled Fielding with Leonard Welsted as an instance of sinking in
verse.   But the foregoing, which he could not have seen,
is scarcely, if at all, inferior to his own *Birthday Poems*
to Stella.[1]

[1] Swift afterwards substituted "the laureate [Cibber]' for
" Fielding," and appears to have changed his mind as to the latter's
merits.   " I can assure Mr. *Fielding*," says Mrs. Pilkington in the

The history of Fielding's marriage rests so exclusively upon the statements of Arthur Murphy that it will be well to quote his words in full :—

"Mr. Fielding had not been long a writer for the stage, when he married Miss Craddock [*sic*], a beauty from Salisbury. About that time, his mother dying, a moderate estate, at Stower in Dorsetshire, devolved to him. To that place he retired with his wife, on whom he doated, with a resolution to bid adieu to all the follies and intemperances to which he had addicted himself in the career of a town-life. But unfortunately a kind of family-pride here gained an ascendant over him ; and he began immediately to vie in splendour with the neighbouring country 'squires. With an estate not much above two hundred pounds a-year, and his wife's fortune, which did not exceed fifteen hundred pounds, he encumbered himself with a large retinue of servants, all clad in costly yellow liveries. For their master's honour, these people could not descend so low as to be careful in their apparel, but, in a month or two, were unfit to be seen ; the 'squire's dignity required that they should be new-equipped ; and his chief pleasure consisting in society and convivial mirth, hospitality threw open his doors, and, in less than three years, entertainments, hounds, and horses, entirely devoured a little patrimony, which, had it been managed with œconomy, might have secured to him a state of independence for the rest of his life, etc."

This passage, which has played a conspicuous part in all biographies of Fielding, was very carefully sifted by Mr. Keightley, who came to the conclusion that it was a "mere tissue of error and inconsistency."[1] Without going to this length, we must admit that it is manifestly

third and last volume of her *Memoirs* (1754), "the Dean had a high opinion of his Wit, which must be a Pleasure to him, as no Man was ever better qualified to judge, possessing it so eminently himself."

[1] Some of Mr. Keightley's criticisms were anticipated by Watson.

incorrect in many respects.	If Fielding married in 1735
(though, as already pointed out, he may have married earlier, and retired to the country upon the failure
of the *Universal Gallant*), he is certainly inaccurately
described as "not having been long a writer for the
stage," since writing for the stage had been his chief
occupation for seven years.	Then again his mother had
died as far back as April 10, 1718, when he was a boy
of eleven; and if he had inherited anything from her, he
had probably been in the enjoyment of it ever since he
came of age.	Furthermore, the statement as to "three
years" is at variance with the fact that, according to the
dedication to the *Universal Gallant*, he was still in London in February 1735, and was back again managing the
Haymarket in the first months of 1736.	Murphy,
however, may only mean that the "estate" at East
Stour was in his possession for three years.	Mr.
Keightley's other points—namely, that the "tolerably
respectable farm-house," in which he is supposed to
have lived, was scarcely adapted to "splendid entertainments," or "a large retinue of servants;" and that, to
be in strict accordance with the family arms, the liveries
should have been not "yellow," but white and blue—must
be taken for what they are worth.	On the whole, the
probability is, that Murphy's words were only the careless repetition of local tittle-tattle, of much of which, as
Captain Booth says pertinently in *Amelia*, "the only
basis is lying."	The squires of the neighbourhood
would naturally regard the dashing young gentleman
from London with the same distrustful hostility that
Addison's "Tory Foxhunter" exhibited to those who
differed with him in politics.	It would be remembered,

besides, that the new-comer was the son of another and
an earlier Fielding of less pretensions, and no real cor-
diality could ever have existed between them. Indeed,
it may be assumed that this was the case, for Booth's
account of the opposition and ridicule which he—" a poor
renter !"—encountered when he enlarged his farm and
set up his coach has a distinct personal accent. That he
was lavish, and lived beyond his means, is quite in accordance with his character. The man who, as a Bow Street
magistrate, kept open house on a pittance, was not likely
to be less lavish as a country gentleman, with £1500 in
his pocket, and newly married to a young and handsome
wife. " He would have wanted money," said Lady Mary,
" if his hereditary lands had been as extensive as his
imagination ; " and there can be little doubt that the
rafters of the old farm by the Stour, with the great locust
tree at the back, which is figured in Hutchins's *History of
Dorset*, rang often to hunting choruses, and that not seldom the " dusky Night rode down the Sky " over the
prostrate forms of Harry Fielding's guests.[1] But even
£1500, and (in spite of Murphy) it is by no means clear
that he had anything more, could scarcely last for ever.
Whether his footmen wore yellow or not, a few brief
months found him again in town. That he was able

---

[1] An interesting relic of the East Stour residence has recently
been presented by Mr. Merthyr Guest (through Mr. R. A. Kinglake)
to the Somersetshire Archæological Society. It is an oak table of
solid proportions, and bears on a brass plate the following inscription, emanating from a former owner :—" This table belonged to
Henry Fielding, Esq., novelist. He hunted from East Stour Farm,
1718, and in three years dissipated his fortune keeping hounds."
In 1718, it may be observed, Fielding was a boy of eleven. Probably the whole of the latter sentence is nothing more than a dis-
tortion of Murphy.

to rent a theatre may perhaps be accepted as proof that
his profuse hospitalities had not completely exhausted
his means.

The moment was a favourable one for a fresh theatrical experiment. The stage-world was split up into
factions, the players were disorganised, and everything
seemed in confusion. Whether Fielding himself conceived the idea of making capital out of this state of
things, or whether it was suggested to him by some of
the company who had acted *Don Quixote in England*,
it is impossible to say. In the first months of 1736,
however, he took the little French Theatre in the
Haymarket, and opened it with a company which he
christened the "Great Mogul's Company of Comedians,"
who were further described as "having dropped from
the Clouds." The "Great Mogul" was a name sometimes given by playwrights to the elder Cibber; but there
is no reason for supposing that any allusion to him was
intended on this occasion. The company, with the exception of Macklin, who was playing at Drury Lane,
consisted chiefly of the actors in *Don Quixote in England;*
and the first piece was entitled *Pasquin : a Dramatick
Satire on the Times : being the Rehearsal of Two Plays, viz. a
Comedy call'd the Election, and a Tragedy call'd the Life and
Death of Common-Sense.* The form of this work, which
belongs to the same class as Sheridan's *Critic* and Buckingham's *Rehearsal*, was probably determined by Fielding's
past experience of the public taste. His latest comedy
had failed, and its predecessors had not been very successful. But his burlesques had met with a better
reception, while the election episodes in *Don Quixote* had
seemed to disclose a fresh field for the satire of con-

temporary manners.   And in the satire of contemporary
manners he felt his strength lay.   The success of *Pasquin*
proved he had not miscalculated, for it ran more than
forty nights, drawing, if we may believe the unknown
author of the life of Theophilus Cibber, numerous and
enthusiastic audiences "from *Grosvenor, Cavendish, Han-
over*, and all the other fashionable Squares, as also from
Pall Mall, and the *Inns of Court*."

In regard to plot, the comedy which *Pasquin* contains
scarcely deserves the name.   It consists of a string of
loosely-connected scenes, which depict the shameless political corruption of the Walpole era with a good deal of
boldness and humour.   The sole difference between the
"Court party," represented by two Candidates with the
Bunyan-like names of Lord Place and Colonel Promise,
and the "Country party," whose nominees are Sir Harry
Fox-Chace and Squire Tankard, is that the former bribe
openly, the latter indirectly.   The Mayor, whose sympathies are with the "Country party" is finally induced by his wife to vote for and return the other side,
although they are in a minority; and the play is concluded by the precipitate marriage of his daughter with
Colonel Promise.   Mr. Fustian, the Tragic Author, who,
with Mr. Sneerwell the Critic, is one of the spectators of
the rehearsal, demurs to the abruptness with which this
ingenious catastrophe is brought about, and inquires
where the preliminary action, of which there is not the
slightest evidence in the piece itself, has taken place.
Thereupon Trapwit, the Comic Author, replies as follows,
in one of those passages which show that, whatever
Fielding's dramatic limitations may have been, he was
at least a keen critic of stage practice :—

" *Trapwit*. Why, behind the Scenes, Sir. What, would you have every Thing brought upon the Stage ? I intend to bring ours to the Dignity of the *French* Stage ; and I have *Horace's* Advice of my Side ; we have many Things both said and done in our Comedies, which might be better perform'd behind the Scenes : The *French*, you know, banish all Cruelty from their Stage ; and I don't see why we should bring on a Lady in ours, practising all manner of Cruelty upon her Lover : beside, Sir, we do not only produce it, but encourage it ; for I could name you some Comedies, if I would, where a Woman is brought in for four Acts together, behaving to a worthy Man in a Manner for which she almost deserves to be hang'd ; and in the Fifth, forsooth, she is rewarded with him for a Husband : Now, Sir, as I know this hits some Tastes, and am willing to oblige all, I have given every Lady a Latitude of thinking mine has behaved in whatever Manner she would have her."

The part of Lord Place in the *Election*, after the first few nights, was taken by Cibber's daughter, the notorious Mrs. Charlotte Charke, whose extraordinary Memoirs are among the curiosities of eighteenth-century literature, and whose experiences were as varied as those of any character in fiction. She does not seem to have acted in the *Life and Death of Common-Sense*, the rehearsal of which followed that of the *Election*. This is a burlesque of the *Tom Thumb* type, much of which is written in vigorous blank verse. Queen Common-Sense is conspired against by Firebrand, Priest of the Sun, by Law, and by Physic. Law is incensed because she has endeavoured to make his piebald jargon intelligible ; Physic because she has preferred Water Gruel to all his drugs ; and Firebrand because she would restrain the power of Priests. Some of the strokes must have gone home to those receptive hearers who, as one contemporary account informs us, " were dull enough

not only to think they contain'd Wit and Humour, but
Truth also ":—

> " *Queen Common-Sense.* My Lord of *Law*, I sent for you
>   this Morning ;
> I have a strange Petition given to me ;
> Two Men, it seems, have lately been at Law
> For an Estate, which both of them have lost,
> And their Attorneys now divide between them.
>   *Law.* Madam, these things will happen in the Law.
>   *Q. C. S.* Will they, my Lord ? then better we had none :
> But I have also heard a sweet Bird sing,
> That Men, unable to discharge their Debts
> At a short Warning, being sued for them,
> Have, with both Power and Will their Debts to pay
> Lain all their Lives in Prison for their Costs.
>   *Law.* That may perhaps be some poor Person's Case,
> Too mean to entertain your Royal Ear.
>   *Q. C. S.* My Lord, while I am Queen I shall not think
> One Man too mean, or poor, to be redress'd ;
> Moreover, Lord, I am inform'd your Laws
> Are grown so large, and daily yet encrease,
> That the great Age of old *Methusalem*
> Would scarce suffice to read your Statutes out."

There is also much more than merely transitory satire
in the speech of "Firebrand" to the Queen :—

> " *Firebrand.* Ha ! do you doubt it ? nay, if you doubt
>   that,
> I will prove nothing—But my zeal inspires me,
> And I will tell you, Madam, you yourself
> Are a most deadly Enemy to the Sun,
> And all his Priests have greatest Cause to wish
> You had been never born.
>   *Q. C. S.* Ha ! say'st thou, Priest ?
> Then know I honour and adore the Sun !
> And when I see his Light, and feel his Warmth,
> I glow with flaming Gratitude toward him ;
> But know, I never will adore a Priest,

> Who wears Pride's Face beneath Religion's Mask,
> And makes a Pick-Lock of his Piety,
> To steal away the Liberty of Mankind.
> But while I live, I'll never give thee Power.
>   *Firebrand.* Madam, our Power is not deriv'd from you,
> Nor any one : 'Twas sent us in a Box
> From the great Sun himself, and Carriage paid ;
> *Phaeton* brought it when he overturn'd
> The Chariot of the Sun into the Sea.
>   *Q. C. S.* Shew me the Instrument, and let me read it.
>   *Fireb.* Madam, you cannot read it, for being thrown
> Into the Sea, the Water has so damag'd it,
> That none but Priests could ever read it since."

In the end, Firebrand stabs Common-Sense, but her Ghost frightens Ignorance off the Stage, upon which Sneerwell says—"I am glad you make *Common-Sense* get the better at last ; I was under terrible Apprehensions for your Moral." "Faith, Sir," says Fustian, "this is almost the only Play where she has got the better lately." And so the piece closes. But it would be wrong to quit it without some reference to the numberless little touches by which, throughout the whole, the humours of dramatic life behind the scenes are ironically depicted. The Comic Poet is arrested on his way from "*King's Coffee-House,*" and the claim being "for upwards of Four Pound," it is at first supposed that "he will hardly get Bail." He is subsequently inquired after by a Gentlewoman in a Riding-Hood, whom he passes off as a Lady of Quality, but who, in reality, is bringing him a clean shirt. There are difficulties with one of the Ghosts, who has a "Church-yard Cough," and "is so Lame he can hardly walk the Stage ;" while another comes to rehearsal without being properly floured, because the stage barber has gone to Drury Lane "to shave the

E

Sultan in the New Entertainment." On the other 1and,
the Ghost of Queen Common-Sense appears before she
is killed, and is with some difficulty persuaded that her
action is premature. Part of "the Mob" play truant to
see a show in the park; Law, straying without the play-
house passage is snapped up by a Lord Chief-Justice's
Warrant; and a Jew carries off one of the Maids of
Honour. These little incidents, together with the un-
blushing realism of the Pots of Porter that are made to
do duty for wine, and the extra two-pennyworth of
Lightning that is ordered against the first night, are all
in the spirit of that inimitable picture of the *Strolling
Actresses dressing in a Barn*, which Hogarth gave to the
world two years later, and which, very possibly, may
have borrowed some of its inspiration from Fielding's
"dramatic satire."

There is every reason to suppose that the profits of
Pasquin were far greater than those of any of its author's
previous efforts. In a rare contemporary caricature,
preserved in the British Museum,[1] the "Queen of
Common-Sense" is shown presenting "Henry Fielding,
Esq.," with a well-filled purse, while to "Harlequin"
(John Rich of Covent Garden) she extends a halter;
and in some doggerel lines underneath, reference is
made to the "show'rs of Gold" resulting from the
piece. This, of course, might be no more than a poetical
fiction; but Fielding himself attests the pecuniary success of *Pasquin* in the Dedication to *Tumble-Down Dick*,
and Mrs. Charke's statement in her Memoirs that her
salary for acting the small part of Lord Place was four
guineas a week, "with an Indulgence in Point of

---

[1] Political and Personal Satires, No. 2287.

Charges at her Benefit" by which she cleared sixty guineas, certainly points to a prosperous exchequer. Fielding's own benefit, as appears from the curious ticket attributed to Hogarth and facsimiled by A. M. Ireland, took place on April 25, but we have no record of the amount of his gains. Mrs. Charke farther says that "soon after *Pasquin* began to droop," Fielding produced Lillo's *Fatal Curiosity* in which she acted Agnes. This tragedy, founded on a Cornish story, is one of remarkable power and passion; but upon its first appearance it made little impression, although in the succeeding year it was acted to greater advantage in combination with another satirical medley by Fielding, the *Historical Register for the Year* 1736.

Like most sequels, the *Historical Register* had neither the vogue nor the wit of its predecessor. It was only half as long, and it was even more disconnected in character. "Harmonious Cibber," as Swift calls him, whose "preposterous Odes" had already been ridiculed in *Pasquin* and the *Author's Farce*, was once more brought on the stage as Ground-Ivy, for his alterations of Shakespeare; and under the name of Pistol, Theophilus Cibber is made to refer to the contention between his second wife, Arne's sister, and Mrs. Clive, for the honour of playing "Polly" in the *Beggar's Opera*, a play-house feud which at the latter end of 1736 had engaged "the Town" almost as seriously as the earlier rivalry of Faustina and Cuzzoni. This continued raillery of the Cibbers is, as Fielding himself seems to have felt, a "Jest a little overacted;" but there is one scene in the piece of undeniable freshness and humour, to wit, that in which Cock, the famous salesman of the Piazzas—the George Robins of

his day—is brought on the stage as Mr. Auctioneer Hen
(a part taken by Mrs. Charke). His wares, "collected
by the indefatigable Pains of that celebrated Virtuoso,
Peter Humdrum, Esq.," include such desirable items as
"curious Remnants of Political Honesty," "delicate
Pieces of Patriotism," Modesty (which does not obtain a
bid), Courage, Wit, and "a very neat clear Conscience"
of great capacity, "which has been worn by a Judge, and
a Bishop." The "Cardinal Virtues" are then put up,
and eighteen-pence is bid for them. But after they have
been knocked down at this extravagant sum, the buyer
complains that he had understood the auctioneer to say
"a Cardinal's Virtues," and that the lot he has purchased
includes "Temperance and Chastity, and a Pack of Stuff
that he would not give three Farthings for." The whole
of this scene is "admirable fooling;" and it was afterwards impudently stolen by Theophilus Cibber for his
farce of the *Auction*. The *Historical Register* concludes
with a dialogue between Quidam, in whom the audience
recognised Sir Robert Walpole, and four patriots, to
whom he gives a purse which has an instantaneous effect
upon their opinions. All five then go off dancing to
Quidam's fiddle; and it is explained that they have holes
in their pockets through which the money will fall as
they dance, enabling the donor to pick it all up again,
"and so not lose one Half-penny by his Generosity."

The frank effrontery of satire like the foregoing had
by this time begun to attract the attention of the
Ministry, whose withers had already been sharply wrung
by *Pasquin;* and it has been conjectured that the ballet
of Quidam and the Patriots played no small part in
precipitating the famous "Licensing Act," which was

passed a few weeks afterwards.   Like the marriage which
succeeded the funeral of Hamlet's father, it certainly
"followed hard upon."   But the reformation of the stage
had already been contemplated by the Legislature ; and
two years before, Sir John Barnard had brought in a
bill "to restrain the number of houses for playing of
Interludes, and for the better regulating of common
Players of Interludes."   This, however, had been abandoned, because it was proposed to add a clause enlarging
the power of the Lord Chamberlain in licensing plays,
an addition to which the introducer of the measure made
strong objection.   He thought the power of the Lord
Chamberlain already too great, and in support of his argument he instanced its wanton exercise in the case of Gay's
Polly, the representation of which had been suddenly
prohibited a few years earlier.   But *Pasquin* and the
Register brought the question of dramatic lawlessness
again to the front, and a bill was hurriedly drawn, one
effect of which was to revive the very provision that
Sir John Barnard had opposed.   The history of this
affair is exceedingly obscure, and in all probability it
has never been completely revealed.   The received or
authorised version is to be found in Coxe's *Life of Walpole*.   After dwelling on the offence given to the Government by *Pasquin*, the writer goes on to say that Giffard,
the manager of Goodman's Fields, brought Walpole a
farce called *The Golden Rump*, which had been proposed for exhibition.   Whether he did this to extort
money, or to ask advice, is not clear.   In either case,
Walpole is said to have "paid the profits which might
have accrued from the performance, and detained the
copy."   He then made a compendious selection of the

treasonable and profane passages it contained. These he submitted to independent members of both parties, and afterwards read them in the House itself. The result was that by way of amendment to the "Vagrant Act" of Anne's reign, a bill was prepared limiting the number of theatres, and compelling all dramatic writers to obtain a license from the Lord Chamberlain. Such is Coxe's account; but notwithstanding its circumstantial character, it has been insinuated in the sham memoirs of the younger Cibber, and it is plainly asserted in the *Rambler's Magazine* for 1787, that certain preliminary details have been conveniently suppressed. It is alleged that Walpole himself caused the farce in question to be written, and to be offered to Giffard, for the purpose of introducing his scheme of reform ; and the suggestion is not without a certain remote plausibility. As may be guessed, however, *The Golden Rump* cannot be appealed to. It was never printed, although its title is identical with that of a caricature published in March 1737, and fully described in the *Gentleman's Magazine* for that month. If the play at all resembled the design, it must have been obscene and scurrilous in the extreme.[1]

Meanwhile the new bill, to which it had given rise, passed rapidly through both Houses. Report speaks of animated discussions and warm opposition. But there are no traces of any divisions, or petitions against it,

[1] Horace Walpole, in his *Memoires of the Last Ten Years of the Reign of George II.*, says (vol. i. p. 12), "I have in my possession the imperfect copy of this piece as I found it among my father's papers after his death." He calls it Fielding's ; but no importance can be attached to the statement. There is a copy of the caricature in the British Museum Print Room (Political and Personal Satires, No. 2327).

and the only speech which has survived is the very
elaborate and careful oration delivered in the Upper
House by Lord Chesterfield. The "second Cicero"—as
Sylvanus Urban styles him—opposed the bill upon the
ground that it would affect the liberty of the press; and
that it was practically a tax upon the chief property of
men of letters, their wit—a "precarious dependence"—
which (he thanked God) my Lords were not obliged to
rely upon. He dwelt also upon the value of the stage
as a fearless censor of vice and folly; and he quoted with
excellent effect but doubtful accuracy the famous answer
of the Prince of Conti [Condé] to Molière [Louis XIV.]
when *Tartuffe* was interdicted at the instance of M. de
Lamoignon:—"It is true, Molière, Harlequin ridicules
Heaven, and exposes religion; but you have done much
worse—you have ridiculed the first minister of religion."
This, although not directly advanced for the purpose,
really indicated the head and front of Fielding's offend-
ing in *Pasquin* and the *Historical Register*, and although in
Lord Chesterfield's speech the former is ironically condemned, it may well be that Fielding, whose *Don Quixote*
had been dedicated to his Lordship, was the wire-puller
in this case, and supplied this very illustration. At all
events it is entirely in the spirit of Firebrand's words in
Pasquin :—

> "Speak boldly ; by the Powers I serve, I swear
> You speak in Safety, even tho' you speak
> Against the Gods, provided that you speak
> Not against Priests."

But the feeling of Parliament in favour of drastic
legislation was even stronger than the persuasive periods

of Chesterfield, and on the 21st of June 1737 the bill
received the royal assent.

With its passing Fielding's career as a dramatic
author practically closed.   In his dedication of the
Historical Register to "the Publick," he had spoken of
his desire to beautify and enlarge his little theatre, and
to procure a better company of actors ; and he had added
—"If Nature hath given me any Talents at ridiculing
Vice and Imposture, I shall not be indolent, nor afraid
of exerting them, while the Liberty of the Press and
Stage subsists, that is to say, while we have any Liberty
left among us."   To all these projects the "Licensing
Act" effectively put an end ; and the only other plays
from his pen which were produced subsequently to this
date were the "Wedding Day," 1743, and the posthumous *Good-Natured Man*, 1779, both of which, as is plain
from the Preface to the *Miscellanies*, were among his
earliest attempts.   In the little farce of *Miss Lucy in Town*,
1742, he had, he says, but "a very small Share."   Besides these, there are three hasty and flimsy pieces which
belong to the early part of 1737.   The first of these,
Tumble-Down Dick ; or, Phaeton in the Suds, was a dramatic sketch in ridicule of the unmeaning Entertainments and Harlequinades of John Rich at Covent
Garden.   This was ironically dedicated to Rich, under
his stage name of "John Lun," and from the dedication
it appears that Rich had brought out an unsuccessful
satire on *Pasquin* called *Marforio*.   The other two were
Eurydice, a profane and pointless farce, afterwards
printed by its author (in anticipation of Beaumarchais)
"as it was d—mned at the Theatre-Royal in Drury-
Lane ;" and a few detached scenes in which, under the

title of *Eurydice Hiss'd ; or, a Word to the Wise*, its untoward fate was attributed to the "frail Promise of
uncertain Friends." But even in these careless and half-
considered productions there are happy strokes ; and
one scarcely looks to find such nervous and sensible lines
in a mere *à propos* as these from *Eurydice Hiss'd :*—

> " Yet grant it shou'd succeed, grant that by Chance,
> Or by the Whim and Madness of the Town,
> A Farce without Contrivance, without Sense
> Should run to the Astonishment of Mankind ;
> Think how you will be read in After-times,
> When Friends are not, and the impartial Judge
> Shall with the meanest Scribbler rank your Name ;
> Who would not rather wish a *Butler's* fame,
> Distress'd, and poor in every thing but Merit,
> Than be the blundering Laureat to a Court ?"

Self-accusatory passages such as this—and there are
others like it — indicate a higher ideal of dramatic
writing than Fielding is held to have attained, and
probably the key to them is to be found in that reaction
of better judgment which seems invariably to have
followed his most reckless efforts. It was a part of
his sanguine and impulsive nature to be as easily persuaded that his work was worthless as that it was
excellent. "When," says Murphy, "he was not under
the immediate urgency of want, they, who were intimate
with him, are ready to aver that he had a mind greatly
superior to anything mean or little ; when his finances
were exhausted, he was not the most elegant in his choice
of the means to redress himself, and he would instantly
exhibit a farce or a puppet-shew in the Haymarket
theatre, which was wholly inconsistent with the profession he had embarked in." The quotation displays all

Murphy's loose and negligent way of dealing with his
facts; for, with the exception of *Miss Lucy in Town*, which
can scarcely be ranked among his works at all, there is
absolutely no trace of Fielding's having exhibited either
"puppet-shew" or "farce" after seriously adopting the
law as a profession, nor does there appear to have been
much acting at the Haymarket for some time after his
management had closed in 1737. Still, his superficial
characteristics, which do not depend so much upon
Murphy as upon those "who were intimate with him,"
are probably accurately described, and they sufficiently
account for many of the obvious discordances of his work
and life. That he was fully conscious of something
higher than his actual achievement as a dramatist is
clear from his own observation in later life, "that he
left off writing for the stage, when he ought to have
begun;"—an utterance which (we shrewdly suspect) has
prompted not a little profitless speculation as to whether,
if he had continued to write plays, they would have been
equal to, or worse than, his novels. The discussion would
be highly interesting, if there were the slightest chance
that it could be attended with any satisfactory result.
But the truth is, that the very materials are wanting.
Fielding "left off writing for the stage" when he was
under thirty; *Tom Jones* was published in 1749, when
he was more than forty. His plays were written in
haste; his novels at leisure, and when, for the most
part, he was relieved from that "immediate urgency of
want," which, according to Murphy, characterised his
younger days. If—as has been suggested—we could
compare a novel written at thirty with a play of the
same date, or a play written at forty with *Tom Jones*,

the comparison might be instructive, although even then considerable allowances would have to be made for the essential difference between plays and novels. But, as we cannot make such a comparison, further inquiry is simply waste of time. All we can safely affirm is, that the plays of Fielding's youth did not equal the fictions of his maturity; and that, of those plays, the comedies were less successful than the farces and burlesques. Among other reasons for this latter difference one chiefly may be given : — that in the comedies he sought to reproduce the artificial world of Congreve and Wycherley, while in the burlesques and farces he depicted the world in which he lived.

CHAPTER III.

THE CHAMPION—JOSEPH ANDREWS.

THE *Historical Register* and *Eurydice Hiss'd* were published together in June 1737. By this time the "Licensing Act" was passed, and the "Grand Mogul's Company" dispersed for ever. Fielding was now in his thirty-first year, with a wife and probably a daughter depending on him for support. In the absence of any prospect that he would be able to secure a maintenance as a dramatic writer, he seems to have decided, in spite of his comparatively advanced age, to revert to the profession for which he had originally been intended, and to qualify himself for the Bar. Accordingly, at the close of the year, he became a student of the Middle Temple, and the books of that society contain the following record of his admission : [1]—

[574 G]   1 *Nov*ris 1737.
*Henricus Fielding, de East Stour in Com Dorset Ar, filius et hœres apparens Brig: Gen*lis *: Edmundi Fielding admissus est in Societatem Medii Templi Lond specialiter et obligatur una cum etc.*

Et dat pro fine 4. 0. 0.

It may be noted, as Mr. Keightley has already

---

[1] This differs slightly from previous transcripts, having been verified at the Middle Temple.

observed, that Fielding is described in this entry as of
East Stour, "which would seem to indicate that he still
retained his property at that place;" and further, that
his father is spoken of as a "brigadier-general," whereas
(according to the *Gentleman's Magazine*) he had been
made a major-general in December 1735.   Of discrepancies like these it is idle to attempt any explanation.   But, if Murphy is to be believed, Fielding devoted
himself henceforth with remarkable assiduity to the
study of law.   The old irregularity of life, it is alleged,
occasionally asserted itself, though without checking the
energy of his application.   "This," says his first biographer, "prevailed in him to such a degree, that he
has been frequently known, by his intimates, to retire
late at night from a tavern to his chambers, and there
read, and make extracts from, the most abstruse authors,
for several hours before he went to bed; so powerful
were the vigour of his constitution and the activity of
his mind."   It is to this passage, no doubt, that we owe
the picturesque wet towel and inked ruffles with which
Mr. Thackeray has decorated him in *Pendennis;* and, in
all probability, a good deal of graphic writing from less
able pens respecting his *modus vivendi* as a Templar.
In point of fact, nothing is known with certainty respecting his life at this period; and what it would really
concern us to learn—namely, whether by "chambers"
it is to be understood that he was living alone, and,
if so, where Mrs. Fielding was at the time of these protracted vigils—Murphy has not told us.   Perhaps she
was safe all the while at East Stour, or with her sisters
at Salisbury.   Having no precise information, however,
it can only be recorded, that, in spite of the fitful

outbreaks above referred to, Fielding applied himself
to the study of his profession with all the vigour of a
man who has to make up for lost time; and that, when
on the 20th of June 1740 the day came for his being
"called," he was very fairly equipped with legal knowledge. That he had also made many friends among his
colleagues of Westminster Hall is manifest from the
number of lawyers who figure in the subscription list of
the *Miscellanies.*

To what extent he was occupied by literary work
during his probationary period it is difficult to say.
Murphy speaks vaguely of "a large number of fugitive
political tracts;" but unless the *Essay on Conversation,*
advertised by Lawton Gilliver in 1737, be the same as
that afterwards reprinted in the *Miscellanies,* there is no
positive record of anything until the issue of *True Greatness,* an epistle to George Dodington, in January 1741,
though he may, of course, have written much anony-
mously. Among newspapers, the one Murphy had in
mind was probably the *Champion,* the first number of
which is dated November 15, 1739, two years after
his admission to the Middle Temple as a student. On
the whole, it seems most likely, as Mr. Keightley conjectures, that his chief occupation in the interval was
studying law, and that he must have been living upon
the residue of his wife's fortune or his own means, in
which case the establishment of the above periodical
may mark the exhaustion of his resources.

The *Champion* is a paper on the model of the elder
essayists. It was issued, like the *Tatler,* on Tuesdays,
Thursdays, and Saturdays. Murphy says that Fielding's
part in it cannot now be ascertained; but as the

"Advertisement" to the edition in two volumes of
1741 states expressly that the papers signed C. and
L. are the "Work of one Hand," and as a number of
those signed C are unmistakably Fielding's, it is hard
to discover where the difficulty lay. The papers signed
C. and L. are by far the most numerous, the majority
of the remainder being distinguished by two stars, or the
signature "Lilbourne." These are understood to have
been from the pen of James Ralph, whose poem of
Night gave rise to a stinging couplet in the *Dunciad*, but
who was nevertheless a man of parts, and an industrious
writer. As will be remembered, he had contributed a
prologue to the *Temple Beau*, so that his association with
Fielding must have been of some standing. Besides
Ralph's essays in the *Champion*, he was mainly responsible
for the *Index to the Times* which accompanied each
number, and consisted of a series of brief paragraphs
on current topics, or the last new book. In this way
Glover's *London*, Boyse's *Deity*, Somervile's *Hobbinol*,
Lillo's *Elmeric*, Dyer's *Ruins of Rome*, and other of the
very minor *poetæ minores* of the day, were commented
upon. These notes and notices, however, were only a
subordinate feature of the *Champion*, which, like its predecessors, consisted chiefly of essays and allegories, social,
moral, and political, the writers of which were supposed
to be members of an imaginary "Vinegar family,"
described in the initial paper. Of these the most prominent was Captain Hercules Vinegar, who took all
questions relating to the Army, Militia, Trained-Bands,
and "fighting Part of the Kingdom." His father,
Nehemiah Vinegar, presided over history and politics;
his uncle, Counsellor Vinegar, over law and judicature;

and Dr. John Vinegar his cousin, over medicine and natural philosophy. To others of the family—including Mrs. Joan Vinegar, who was charged with domestic affairs—were allotted classic literature, poetry and the Drama, and fashion. This elaborate scheme was not very strictly adhered to, and the chief writer of the group is Captain Hercules.

Shorn of the contemporary interest which formed the chief element of its success when it was first published, it must be admitted that, in the present year of grace, the *Champion* is hard reading. A kind of lassitude—a sense of uncongenial task-work—broods heavily over Fielding's contributions, except the one or two in which he is quickened into animation by his antagonism to Cibber; and although, with our knowledge of his after achievements, it is possible to trace some indications of his yet unrevealed powers, in the absence of such knowledge it would be difficult to distinguish the *Champion* from the hundred-and-one forgotten imitators of the *Spectator* and *Tatler*, whose names have been so patiently chronicled by Dr. Nathan Drake. There is, indeed, a certain obvious humour in the account of Captain Vinegar's famous club, which he had inherited from Hercules, and which had the enviable property of falling of itself upon any knave in company, and there is a dash of the *Tom Jones* manner in the noisy activity of that excellent housewife Mrs. Joan. Some of the lighter papers, such as the one upon the "Art of Puffing," are amusing enough; and of the visions, that which is based upon Lucian, and represents Charon as stripping his freight of all their superfluous incumbrances in order to lighten his boat, has a double

interest, since it contains references not only to Cibber,
but also (though this appears to have been hitherto
overlooked) to Fielding himself. The "tall Man," who
at Mercury's request strips off his "old Grey Coat with
great Readiness," but refuses to part with "half his
Chin," which the shepherd of souls regards as false,
is clearly intended for the writer of the paper, even
without the confirmation afforded by the subsequent
allusions to his connection with the stage. His "length
of chin and nose," sufficiently apparent in his portrait,
was a favourite theme for contemporary personalities.
Of the moral essays, the most remarkable are a set of
four papers, entitled *An Apology for the Clergy*, which
may perhaps be regarded as a set-off against the sarcasms
of *Pasquin* on priestcraft. They depict, with a great
deal of knowledge and discrimination, the pattern priest
as Fielding conceived him. To these may be linked an
earlier picture, taken from life, of a country parson who,
in his simple and dignified surroundings, even more
closely resembles the Vicar of Wakefield than Mr.
Abraham Adams. Some of the more general articles
contain happy passages. In one there is an admirable
parody of the Norman-French jargon, which in those
days added superfluous obscurity to legal utterances;
while another, on "Charity," contains a forcible exposition of the inexpediency, as well as inhumanity, of
imprisonment for debt. References to contemporaries,
the inevitable Cibber excepted, are few, and these seem
mostly from the pen of Ralph. The following, from
that of Fielding, is notable as being one of the earliest
authoritative testimonies to the merits of Hogarth : "I
esteem (says he) the ingenious *Mr. Hogarth* as one of

the most useful Satyrists any Age hath produced. In
his excellent Works you see the delusive Scene exposed
with all the Force of Humour, and, on casting your
Eyes on another Picture, you behold the dreadful and
fatal Consequence. I almost dare affirm that those two
Works of his, which he calls the *Rake's* and the *Harlot's
Progress*, are calculated more to serve the Cause of
Virtue, and for the Preservation of Mankind, than all
the *Folio's* of Morality which have been ever written;
and a sober Family should no more be without them,
than without the *Whole Duty of Man* in their House."
He returned to the same theme in the Preface to *Joseph
Andrews* with a still apter phrase of appreciation :—
"It hath been thought a vast Commendation of a
Painter, to say his Figures seem to breathe ; but surely,
it is a much greater and nobler Applause, that they
appear to think." [1]

When the *Champion* was rather more than a year
old, Colley Cibber published his famous *Apology*. To
the attacks made upon him by Fielding at different times
he had hitherto printed no reply—perhaps he had no
opportunity of doing so. But in his eighth chapter,
when speaking of the causes which led to the Licensing
Act, he takes occasion to refer to his assailant in terms
which Fielding must have found exceedingly galling.
He carefully abstained from mentioning his name, on
the ground that it could do him no good, and was of

[1] Fielding occasionally refers to Hogarth for the pictorial types
of his characters. Bridget Allworthy, he tells us, resembled the
starched prude in *Morning;* and Mrs. Partridge and Parson
Thwackum have their originals in the *Harlot's Progress.* It was
Fielding, too, who said that the *Enraged Musician* was "enough
to make a man deaf to look at" (*Voyage to Lisbon,* 1755, p. 50).

no importance; but he described him as "a broken
Wit," who had sought notoriety "by raking the Chan-
nel" (*i.e.* Kennel), and "pelting his Superiors." He
accused him, with a scandalised gravity that is as edifying as Chesterfield's irony, of attacking "Religion,
Laws, Government, Priests, Judges, and Ministers."
He called him, either in allusion to his stature, or
his pseudonym in the *Champion*, a "*Herculean* Satyrist,"
a "*Drawcansir* in Wit"—"who, to make his Poetical
Fame immortal, like another *Erostratus*, set Fire to
his Stage, by writing up to an Act of Parliament to
demolish it.   I shall not," he continues, "give the
particular Strokes of his Ingenuity a Chance to be remembered, by reciting them; it may be enough to say,
in general Terms, they were so openly flagrant, that the
Wisdom of the Legislature thought it high time, to take
a proper Notice of them."

Fielding was not the man to leave such a challenge
unanswered.   In the *Champion* for April 22, 1740, and
two subsequent papers, he replied with a slashing criticism of the *Apology*, in which, after demonstrating that
it must be written in English because it was written
in no other language, he gravely proceeds to point out
examples of the author's superiority to grammar and
learning—and in general, subjects its pretentious and
slip-shod style to a minute and highly detrimental
examination.   In a further paper he returns to the
charge by a mock trial of one "Col. *Apol.*" (*i.e.* Colley-
Apology), arraigning him for that, "not having the Fear
of Grammar before his Eyes," he had committed an
unpardonable assault upon his mother-tongue.   Fielding's knowledge of legal forms and phraseology enabled

him to make a happy parody of court procedure, and
Mr. Lawrence says that this particular "*jeu d'esprit* obtained great celebrity." But the happiest stroke in the
controversy—as it seems to us—is one which escaped
Mr. Lawrence, and occurs in the paper already referred
to, where Charon and Mercury are shown denuding the
luckless passengers by the Styx of their surplus *impedi-
menta*. Among the rest, approaches "an elderly Gentleman with a Piece of wither'd Laurel on his head."
From a little book, which he is discovered (when
stripped) to have bound close to his heart, and which
bears the title of *Love in a Riddle* — an unsuccessful
pastoral produced by Cibber at Drury Lane in 1729—
it is clear that this personage is intended for none other
than the Apologist, who, after many entreaties, is finally
compelled to part with his treasure. "I was surprized,"
continues Fielding, "to see him pass Examination with
his Laurel on, and was assured by the Standers by, that
Mercury would have taken it off, if he had seen it."

These attacks in the *Champion* do not appear to have
received any direct response from Cibber. But they
were reprinted in a rambling production issued from
"Curll's chaste press" in 1740, and entitled the *Tryal
of Colley Cibber, Comedian,* &c. At the end of this there
is a short address to "*the Self-dubb'd Captain* Hercules
Vinegar, *alias* Buffoon," to the effect that "the malevolent
Flings exhibited by him and his Man *Ralph*," have been
faithfully reproduced. Then comes the following curious
and not very intelligible "Advertisement : "—

"If the Ingenious *Henry Fielding* Esq.; (Son of the Hon.
Lieut. General *Fielding*, who upon his Return from his
Travels entered himself of the *Temple* in order to study the

Law, and married one of the pretty Miss *Cradocks* of *Salisbury*)
will *own* himself the AUTHOR of 18 strange Things called
Tragical *Comedies* and Comical *Tragedies*, lately advertised by
J. *Watts*, of *Wild-Court*, Printer, he shall be *mentioned* in
Capitals in the *Third* Edition of Mr. CIBBER's *Life*, and likewise be placed *among* the *Poetæ minores Dramatici* of the
Present Age : Then will both his *Name and Writings be
remembered on Record* in the immortal *Poetical Register*
written by Mr. GILES JACOB."

The "poetical register" indicated was the book of
that name, containing the *Lives and Characteristics of
the English Dramatic Poets*, which Mr. Giles Jacob, an
industrious literary hack, had issued in 1723.   Mr.
Lawrence is probably right in his supposition, based upon
the foregoing advertisement, that Fielding "had openly
expressed resentment at being described by Cibber as 'a
broken wit,' without being mentioned by name."   He
never seems to have wholly forgotten his animosity to
the actor, to whom there are frequent references in
Joseph Andrews ; and, as late as 1749, he is still found
harping on "the withered laurel" in a letter to Lyttelton.   Even in his last work, the *Voyage to Lisbon*, Cibber's
name is mentioned.   The origin of this protracted feud
is obscure ; but, apart from want of sympathy, it must
probably be sought for in some early misunderstanding
between the two in their capacities of manager and
author.   As regards Theophilus Cibber, his desertion
of Highmore was sufficient reason for the ridicule cast
upon him in the *Author's Farce* and elsewhere.   With
Mrs. Charke, the Laureate's intractable and eccentric
daughter, Fielding was naturally on better terms.   She
was, as already stated, a member of the Great Mogul's
Company, and it is worth noting that some of the sar-

casms in *Pasquin* against her father were put into the
mouth of Lord Place, whose part was taken by this un-
dutiful child.   All things considered, both in this controversy and the later one with Pope, Cibber did not
come off worst.   His few hits were personal and unscrupulous, and they were probably far more deadly
in their effects than any of the ironical attacks which
his adversaries, on their part, directed against his poetical ineptitude or halting "parts of speech."   Despite his
superlative coxcombry and egotism, he was, moreover, a
man of no mean abilities.   His *Careless Husband* is a far
better acting play than any of Fielding's, and his *Apology*,
which even Johnson allowed to be "well-done," is valuable in many respects, especially for its account of the
contemporary stage.   In describing an actor or actress
he had few equals—witness his skilful portrait of Nokes,
and his admirably graphic vignette of Mrs. Verbruggen
as that "finish'd Impertinent," Melantha, in Dryden's
Marriage à-la-Mode.

The concluding paper in the collected edition of the
Champion, published in 1741, is dated June 19, 1740.
On the day following Fielding was called to the Bar
by the benchers of the Middle Temple, and (says Mr.
Lawrence) "chambers were assigned him in Pump Court."
Simultaneously with this, his regular connection with
journalism appears to have ceased, although from his
statement in the Preface to the *Miscellanies*,—that "as
long as from *June* 1741," he had "desisted from writing
one Syllable in the *Champion*, or any other public Paper,"
—it may perhaps be inferred that up to that date he
continued to contribute now and then.   This, nevertheless, is by no means clear.   His last utterance in the pub-

lished volumes is certainly in a sense valedictory, as it refers to the position acquired by the *Champion*, and the difficulty experienced in establishing it.   Incidentally, it pays a high compliment to Pope, by speaking of "the divine Translation of the *Iliad*, which he [Fielding] has lately with *no Disadvantage to the Translator* COMPARED with the Original," the point of the sentence so impressed by its typography, being apparently directed against those critics who had condemned Pope's work without the requisite knowledge of Greek.   From the tenor of the rest of the essay it may, however, be concluded that the writer was taking leave of his enterprise ; and, according to a note by Boswell, in his *Life of Johnson*, it seems that Mr. Reed of Staple Inn possessed documents which showed that Fielding at this juncture, probably in anticipation of more lucrative legal duties, surrendered the reins to Ralph.   The *Champion* continued to exist for some time longer ; indeed, it must be regarded as long-lived among the essayists, since the issue which contained its well-known criticism on Garrick is No. 455, and appeared late in 1742.   But as far as can be ascertained, it never again obtained the honours of a reprint.

Although, after he was called to the Bar, Fielding practically relinquished periodical literature, he does not seem to have entirely desisted from writing.   In Sylvanus Urban's Register of Books, published during January 1741, is advertised the poem *Of True Greatness* afterwards included in the *Miscellanies ;* and the same authority announces the *Vernoniad*, an anonymous burlesque Epic prompted by Admiral Vernon's popular expedition against Porto Bello in 1739, "with six Ships

only." That Fielding was the author of the latter is
sufficiently proved by his order to Mr. Nourse (printed
in Roscoe's edition), to deliver fifty copies to Mr Chappel.
Another sixpenny pamphlet, entitled *The Opposition, a
Vision*, issued in December of the same year, is enumerated by him, in the Preface to the *Miscellanies*,
among the few works he had published "since the
End of *June* 1741 ;" and, provided it can be placed
before this date, he may be credited with a political
sermon called the *Crisis* (1741), which is ascribed to him
upon the authority of a writer in Nichols's *Anecdotes.* He
may also, before "the End of *June* 1741," have written
other things ; but it is clear from his *Caveat* in the
above-mentioned " Preface," together with his complaint
that "he had been very unjustly censured, as well on
account of what he had not writ, as for what he had,"
that much more has been laid to his charge than he ever
deserved.   Among ascriptions of this kind may be
mentioned the curious *Apology for the Life of Mr. The
Cibber, Comedian*, 1740, which is described on its title-page
as a proper sequel to the autobiography of the Laureate,
in whose "style and manner" it is said to be written.
But, although this performance is evidently the work of
some one well acquainted with the dramatic annals of
the day, it is more than doubtful whether Fielding had
any hand or part in it.   Indeed, his own statement that
"he never was, nor would be the Author of *anonymous*
Scandal [the italics are ours] on the private History or
Family of any Person whatever," should be regarded as
conclusive.
    During all this time he seems to have been steadily
applying himself to the practice of his profession, if,

indeed, that weary hope deferred which forms the usual probation of legal preferment can properly be so described.   As might be anticipated from his Salisbury connections, he travelled the Western Circuit; and, according to Hutchins's *Dorset*, he assiduously attended the Wiltshire sessions.   He had many friends among his brethren of the Bar.   His cousin, Henry Gould, who had been called in 1734, and who, like his grand-father, ultimately became a Judge, was also a member of the Middle Temple; and he was familiar with Charles Pratt, afterwards Lord Camden, whom he may have known at Eton, but whom he certainly knew in his bar-rister days.   It is probable, too, that he was acquainted with Lord Northington, then Robert Henley, whose name appears as a subscriber to the *Miscellanies*, and who was once supposed to contend with Kettleby (another subscriber) for the honour of being the original of the drunken barrister in Hogarth's *Midnight Modern Conversation*, a picture which no doubt accurately repre-sents a good many of the festivals by which Henry Fielding relieved the tedium of composing those MS. *folio* volumes on Crown or Criminal Law, which, after his death, reverted to his half-brother, Sir John.   But to-wards the close of 1741 he was engaged upon another work which has outweighed all his most laborious foren-sic efforts, and which will long remain an English classic. This was *The History of the Adventures of Joseph Andrews, and of his Friend Mr. Abraham Adams*, published by Andrew Millar in February 1742.

In the same number, and at the same page of the *Gentleman's Magazine* which contains the advertisement of the *Vernoniad*, there is a reference to a famous novel

which had appeared in November 1740, two months
earlier, and had already attained an extraordinary
popularity. "Several Encomiums (says Mr. Urban) on
a Series of *Familiar Letters*, publish'd but last month,
entitled PAMELA or *Virtue rewarded*, came too late for
this Magazine, and we believe there will be little Occasion for inserting them in our next; because a Second
Edition will then come out to supply the Demands in
the Country, it being judged in Town as great a Sign of
Want of Curiosity not to have read *Pamela*, as not to have
seen the *French* and *Italian* Dancers." A second edition
was in fact published in the following month (February),
to be speedily succeeded by a third in March and a
fourth in May. Dr. Sherlock (oddly misprinted by Mrs.
Barbauld as "Dr. Slocock") extolled it from the pulpit;
and the great Mr. Pope was reported to have gone
farther and declared that it would "do more good than
many volumes of sermons." Other admirers ranked it
next to the Bible; clergymen dedicated theological
treatises to the author; and "even at Ranelagh"—says
Richardson's biographer—"those who remember the
publication say, that it was usual for ladies to hold up
the volumes of Pamela to one another, to shew that they
had got the book that every one was talking of." It is
perhaps hypercritical to observe that Ranelagh Gardens
were not opened until eighteen months after Mr. Riving-
ton's *duodecimos* first made their appearance; but it
will be gathered from the tone of some of the foregoing commendations that its morality was a strong
point with the new candidate for literary fame; and
its voluminous title-page did indeed proclaim at large
that it was "Published in order to cultivate the Prin-

ciples of Virtue and Religion in the Minds of the Youth of Both Sexes." Its author, Samuel Richardson, was a middle-aged London printer, a vegetarian and water-drinker, a worthy, domesticated, fussy, and highly-nervous little man. Delighting in female society, and accustomed to act as confidant and amanuensis for the young women of his acquaintance, it had been sug-gested to him by some bookseller friends that he should prepare a "little volume of Letters, in a common style, on such subjects as might be of use to those country readers, who were unable to indite for themselves." As Hogarth's Conversation Pieces grew into his Pro-gresses, so this project seems to have developed into *Pamela, or Virtue Rewarded.* The necessity for some connecting link between the letters suggested a story, and the story chosen was founded upon the actual ex-periences of a young servant girl, who, after victoriously resisting all the attempts made by her master to seduce her, ultimately obliged him to marry her. It is needless to give any account here of the minute and deliber-ate way in which Richardson filled in this outline. As one of his critics, D'Alembert, has unanswerably said— "*La nature est bonne à imiter, mais non pas jusqu'à l'ennui,*" —and the author of *Pamela* has plainly disregarded this useful law. On the other hand, the tedium and elaboration of his style have tended, in these less leisurely days, to condemn his work to a neglect which it does not deserve. Few writers—it is a truism to say so—have excelled him in minute analysis of motive, and knowledge of the human heart. About the final morality of his heroine's long-drawn defence of her chastity it may, however, be permitted to doubt; and,

in contrasting the book with Fielding's work, it should
not be forgotten that, irreproachable though it seemed to
the author's admirers, good Dr. Watts complained (and
with reason) of the indelicacy of some of the scenes.

But, for the moment, we are more concerned with the
effect which *Pamela* produced upon Henry Fielding,
struggling with the "eternal want of pence, which vexes
public men," and vaguely hoping for some profitable opening for powers which had not yet been satisfactorily exercised.   To his robust and masculine genius, never very
delicately sensitive where the relations of the sexes are
concerned, the strange conjunction of purity and precau-
tion in Richardson's heroine was a thing unnatural, and
a theme for inextinguishable Homeric laughter.   That
Pamela, through all her trials, could really have cherished
any affection for her unscrupulous admirer would seem
to him a sentimental absurdity, and the unprecedented
success of the book would sharpen his sense of its
assailable side.   Possibly, too, his acquaintance with
Richardson, whom he knew personally, but with whom
he could have had no kind of sympathy, disposed him
against his work.   In any case, the idea presently
occurred to Fielding of depicting a young man in circumstances of similar importunity at the hands of a
dissolute woman of fashion.   He took for his hero
Pamela's brother, and by a malicious stroke of the pen
turned the Mr. B. of *Pamela* into Squire Booby.   But
the process of invention rapidly carried him into paths
far beyond the mere parody of Richardson, and it is only
in the first portion of the book that he really remembers
his intention.   After chapter x. the story follows its
natural course, and there is little or nothing of Lady

Booby, or her frustrate amours. Indeed, the author
does not even pretend to preserve congruity as regards
his hero, for, in chapter v., he makes him tell his mistress
that he has never been in love, while in chapter xi. we
are informed that he had long been attached to the
charming Fanny. Moreover, in the intervening letters
which Joseph writes to his sister Pamela, he makes no
reference to this long-existent attachment, with which,
one would think, she must have been perfectly familiar.
These discrepancies all point, not so much to negligence
on the part of the author, as to an unconscious transformation of his plan. He no doubt speedily found that
mere ridicule of Richardson was insufficient to sustain
the interest of any serious effort, and, besides, must
have been secretly conscious that the " Pamela " characteristics of his hero were artistically irreconcilable with
the personal bravery and cudgel-playing attributes with
which he had endowed him. Add to this that the
immortal Mrs. Slipslop and Parson Adams — the
latter especially—had begun to acquire an importance
with their creator for which the initial scheme had by no
means provided ; and he finally seems to have disregarded his design, only returning to it in his last chapters
in order to close his work with some appearance of consistency. The *History of Joseph Andrews*, it has been
said, might well have dispensed with Lady Booby alto-
gether, and yet, without her, not only this book, but
Tom Jones and *Amelia* also, would probably have been
lost to us. The accident which prompted three such
masterpieces cannot be honestly regretted.

It was not without reason that Fielding added promi-
nently to his title-page the name of Mr. Abraham Adams.

If he is not the real hero of the book, he is undoubtedly
the character whose fortunes the reader follows with the
closest interest. Whether he is smoking his black and
consolatory pipe in the gallery of the inn, or losing his way
while he dreams over a passage of Greek, or groaning
over the fatuities of the man-of-fashion in Leonora's story,
or brandishing his famous crabstick in defence of Fanny,
he is always the same delightful mixture of benevolence
and simplicity, of pedantry and credulity and ignorance
of the world. He is "compact," to use Shakespeare's
word, of the oddest contradictions,—the most diverting
eccentricities. He has Aristotle's *Politics* at his fingers'
ends, but he knows nothing of the daily *Gazetteers ;* he
is perfectly familiar with the Pillars of Hercules, but
he has never even heard of the Levant. He travels to
London to sell a collection of sermons which he has forgotten to carry with him, and in a moment of excitement
he tosses into the fire the copy of *Æschylus* which it has
cost him years to transcribe. He gives irreproachable
advice to Joseph on fortitude and resignation, but he
is overwhelmed with grief when his child is reported to
be drowned. When he speaks upon faith and works,
on marriage, on school discipline, he is weighty and
sensible ; but he falls an easy victim to the plausible
professions of every rogue he meets, and is willing to
believe in the principles of Mr. Peter Pounce, or the
humanity of Parson Trulliber. Not all the discipline
of hog's blood and cudgels and cold water to which he is
subjected can deprive him of his native dignity ; and
as he stands before us in the short great-coat under
which his ragged cassock is continually making its
appearance, with his old wig and battered hat, a clergy-

man whose social position is scarcely above that of a
footman, and who supports a wife and six children upon
a cure of twenty-three pounds a year, which his out-
spoken honesty is continually jeopardising, he is a far
finer figure than Pamela in her coach-and-six, or
Bellarmine in his cinnamon velvet. If not, as Mr.
Lawrence says, with exaggerated enthusiasm, "the
grandest delineation of a pattern-priest which the world
has yet seen," he is assuredly a noble example of primi-
tive goodness and practical Christianity. It is certain—
as Mr. Forster and Mr. Keightley have pointed out—
that Goldsmith borrowed some of his characteristics for
Dr. Primrose, and it has been suggested that Sterne remembered him in more than one page of *Tristram Shandy*.

Next to Parson Adams, perhaps the best character in
Joseph Andrews—though of an entirely different type—
is Lady Booby's "Waiting-Gentlewoman," the excellent
Mrs. Slipslop. Her sensitive dignity, her easy changes
from servility to insolence, her sensuality, her inimitably
distorted vocabulary, which Sheridan borrowed for Mrs.
Malaprop, and Dickens modified for Mrs. Gamp, are
all peculiarities which make up a personification of the
richest humour and the most life-like reality. Mr. Peter
Pounce, too, with his "scoundrel maxims," as disclosed
in that remarkable dialogue which is said to be "better
worth reading than all the Works of *Colley Cibber*," and
in which charity is defined as consisting rather in a disposition to relieve distress than in an actual act of relief;
Parson Trulliber with his hogs, his greediness, and his
willingness to prove his Christianity by fisticuffs;
shrewish Mrs. Tow-wouse with her scold's tongue, and
her erring but perfectly subjugated husband,—these

again are portraits finished with admirable spirit and
fidelity.   Andrews himself, and his blushing sweetheart,
do not lend themselves so readily to humorous art.
Nevertheless the former, when freed from the wiles of
Lady Booby, is by no means a despicable hero, and
Fanny is a sufficiently fresh and blooming heroine.   The
characters of Pamela and Mr. Booby are fairly preserved
from the pages of their original inventor.   But when
Fielding makes Parson Adams rebuke the pair for
laughing in church at Joseph's wedding, and puts into
the lady's mouth a sententious little speech upon her
altered position in life, he is adding some ironical touches
which Richardson would certainly have omitted.

No selection of personages, however, even of the
most detailed and particular description, can convey any
real impression of the mingled irony and insight, the
wit and satire, the genial but perfectly remorseless re-
velation of human springs of action, which distinguish
scene after scene of the book.   Nothing, for example,
can be more admirable than the different manifestations
of meanness which take place among the travellers of
the stage-coach, in the oft-quoted chapter where Joseph,
having been robbed of everything, lies naked and bleed-
ing in the ditch.   There is Miss Grave-airs, who protests
against the indecency of his entering the vehicle, but
like a certain lady in the *Rake's Progress*, holds the sticks
of her fan before her face while he does so, and who is
afterwards found to be carrying Nantes under the guise
of Hungary-water ; there is the lawyer who advises that
the wounded man shall be taken in, not from any
humane motive, but because he is afraid of being involved in legal proceedings if they leave him to his fate ;

there is the wit who seizes the occasion for a burst of
facetious *double-entendres*, chiefly designed for the dis-
comfiture of the prude; and, lastly, there is the coachman,
whose only concern is the shilling for his fare, and who
refuses to lend either of the useless greatcoats he is
sitting upon, lest "they should be made bloody," leaving
the shivering suppliant to be clothed by the generosity
of the postilion ("a Lad," says Fielding with a fine touch
of satire, "who hath been since transported for robbing
a Hen-roost"). This worthy fellow accordingly strips
off his only outer garment, "at the same time swearing
a great Oath," for which he is duly rebuked by the
passengers, "that he would rather ride in his Shirt all
his Life, than suffer a Fellow-Creature to lie in so
miserable a Condition." Then there are the admirable
scenes which succeed Joseph's admission into the inn ;
the discussion between the bookseller and the two
parsons as to the publication of Adams's sermons, which
the "Clergy would be certain to cry down," because
they inculcate good works against faith ; the debate
before the justice as to the manuscript of Æschylus,
which is mistaken for one of the Fathers ; and the pleasant
discourse between the poet and the player which, beginning by compliments, bids fair to end in blows.
Nor are the stories of Leonora and Mr. Wilson without
their interest. They interrupt the straggling narrative
far less than the Man of the Hill interrupts *Tom
Jones*, and they afford an opportunity for varying the epic
of the highway by pictures of polite society which could
not otherwise be introduced. There can be little doubt,
too, that some of Mr. Wilson's town experiences were
the reflection of the author's own career; while the charac-

G

teristics of Leonora's lover Horatio,—who was "a young
Gentleman of a good Family, bred to the Law," and recently called to the Bar, whose "Face and Person were
such as the Generality allowed handsome : but he had
a Dignity in his Air very rarely to be seen," and who
"had Wit and Humour, with an Inclination to Satire,
which he indulged rather too much"—read almost like
a complimentary description of Fielding himself.

Like Hogarth, in that famous drinking scene to
which reference has already been made, Fielding was
careful to disclaim any personal portraiture in *Joseph
Andrews*. In the opening chapter of Book iii. he
declares "once for all that he describes not Men, but
Manners ; not an Individual, but a Species," although
he admits that his characters are "taken from Life."
In his "Preface," he reiterates this profession, adding
that in copying from nature, he has "used the utmost
Care to obscure the Persons by such different Circumstances, Degrees, and Colours, that it will be impossible
to guess at them with any degree of certainty." Nevertheless—as in Hogarth's case—neither his protests nor
his skill have prevented some of those identifications
which are so seductive to the curious ; and it is generally believed,—indeed, it was expressly stated by
Richardson and others,—that the prototype of Parson
Adams was a friend of Fielding, the Reverend William
Young. Like Adams, he was a scholar and devoted to
Æschylus ; he resembled him, too, in his trick of snap-
ping his fingers, and his habitual absence of mind. Of
this latter peculiarity it is related that on one occasion,
when a chaplain in Marlborough's wars, he strolled
abstractedly into the enemy's lines with his beloved

Æschylus in his hand. His peaceable intentions were so unmistakable that he was instantly released, and politely directed to his regiment. Once, too, it is said, on being charged by a gentleman with sitting for the portrait of Adams, he offered to knock the speaker down, thereby supplying additional proof of the truth of the allegation. He died in August 1757, and is buried in the Chapel of Chelsea Hospital. The obituary notice in the *Gentleman's Magazine* describes him as "late of Gillingham, Dorsetshire," which would make him a neighbour of the novelist.[1] Another tradition connects Mr. Peter Pounce with the scrivener and usurer Peter Walter, whom Pope had satirised, and whom Hogarth is thought to have introduced into Plate i. of Marriage *à-la-Mode.* His sister lived at Salisbury ; and he himself had an estate at Stalbridge Park, which was close to East Stour. From references to Walter in the *Champion* for May 31, 1740, as well as in the *Essay on Conversation,* it is clear that Fielding knew him personally, and disliked him. He may, indeed, have been among those county magnates whose criticism was so objectionable to Captain Booth during his brief residence in Dorsetshire. Parson Trulliber, also, according to Murphy, was Fielding's first tutor —Mr. Oliver of Motcombe. But his widow denied the resemblance ; and it is hard to believe that this portrait is not overcharged. In all these cases, however, there is no reason for supposing that Fielding may not have thoroughly believed in the sincerity of his attempts to avoid the exact reproduction of actual persons, although, rightly or wrongly, his present-

[1] Lord Thurlow was accustomed to find a later likeness to Fielding's hero in his *protégé*, the poet Crabbe.

ments were speedily identified. With ordinary people
it is by salient characteristics that a likeness is established; and no variation of detail, however skilful, greatly
affects this result. In our own days we have seen
that, in spite of both authors, the public declined to
believe that the Harold Skimpole of Charles Dickens,
and George Eliot's Dinah Morris, were not perfectly
recognisable copies of living originals.

Upon its title-page, *Joseph Andrews* is declared to be
" written in Imitation of the Manner of Cervantes," and
there is no doubt that, in addition to being subjected to
an unreasonable amount of ill-usage, Parson Adams
has manifest affinities with Don Quixote. Scott, however, seems to have thought that Scarron's *Roman
Comique* was the real model, so far as mock-heroic
was concerned ; but he must have forgotten that Fielding was already the author of *Tom Thumb*, and that
Swift had written the *Battle of the Books.* Resemblances
—not of much moment—have also been traced to the
Paysan Parvenu and the *Histoire de Marianne* of Marivaux. With both these books Fielding was familiar ; in
fact, he expressly mentions them, as well as the *Roman
Comique*, in the course of his story, and they doubtless
exercised more or less influence upon his plan. But in
the Preface, from which we have already quoted, he
describes that plan ; and this, because it is something
definite, is more interesting than any speculation as to
his determining models. After marking the division of
the Epic, like the Drama, into Tragedy and Comedy, he
points out that it may exist in prose as well as verse,
and he proceeds to explain that what he has attempted
in *Joseph Andrews* is " a comic Epic-Poem in Prose,"

differing from serious romance in its substitution of a light and ridiculous" fable for a "grave and solemn" one, of inferior characters for those of superior rank, and of ludicrous for sublime sentiments. Sometimes in the diction he has admitted burlesque, but never in the sentiments and characters, where, he contends, it would be out of place. He further defines the only source of the ridiculous to be affectation, of which the chief causes are vanity and hypocrisy. Whether this scheme was an after-thought it is difficult to say; but it is certainly necessary to a proper understanding of the author's method — a method which was to find so many imitators. Another passage in the Preface is worthy of remark. With reference to the pictures of vice which the book contains, he observes : "First, That it is very difficult to pursue a Series of human Actions, and keep clear from them. Secondly, That the Vices to be found here [*i.e.* in *Joseph Andrews*] are rather the accidental Consequences of some human Frailty, or Foible, than Causes habitually existing in the Mind. Thirdly, That they are never set forth as the Objects of Ridicule but Detestation. Fourthly, That they are never the principal Figure at the Time on the Scene ; and, lastly, they never produce the intended Evil." In reading some pages of Fielding it is not always easy to see that he has strictly adhered to these principles ; but it is well to recall them occasionally, as constituting at all events the code that he desired to follow.

Although the popularity of Fielding's first novel was considerable, it did not, to judge by the number of editions, at once equal the popularity of the book by which it was suggested. *Pamela*, as we have seen,

speedily ran through four editions; but it was six
months before Millar published the second and revised
edition of *Joseph Andrews;* and the third did not
appear until more than a year after the date of first
publication.　With Richardson, as might be expected,
it was never popular at all, and to a great extent it
is possible to sympathise with his annoyance.　The
daughter of his brain, whom he had piloted through so
many troubles, had grown to him more real than the
daughters of his body, and to see her at the height of her
fame made contemptible by what in one of his letters he
terms " a lewd and ungenerous engraftment," must have
been a sore trial to his absorbed and self-conscious
nature, and one which not all the consolations of his
consistory of feminine flatterers — "my ladies," as the
little man called them—could wholly alleviate.　But it
must be admitted that his subsequent attitude was
neither judicious nor dignified.　He pursued Fielding
henceforth with steady depreciation, caught eagerly at
any scandal respecting him, professed himself unable
to perceive his genius, deplored his "lowness," and
comforted himself by reflecting that, if he pleased at
all, it was because he had learned the art from *Pamela*.
Of Fielding's other contemporary critics, one only need
be mentioned here, more on account of his literary
eminence than of the special felicity of his judgment.
" I have myself," writes Gray to West, " upon your
recommendation, been reading Joseph Andrews.　The
incidents are ill laid and without invention; but the
characters have a great deal of nature, which always
pleases even in her lowest shapes.　Parson Adams is
perfectly well; so is Mrs. Slipslop, and the story of

Wilson; and throughout he [*the author*] shews himself
well read in Stage-Coaches, Country Squires, Inns, and
Inns of Court. His reflections upon high people and
low people, and misses and masters, are very good.
However the exaltedness of some minds (or rather as I
shrewdly suspect their insipidity and want of feeling or
observation) may make them insensible to these light
things, (I mean such as characterise and paint nature)
yet surely they are as weighty and much more useful
than your grave discourses upon the mind, the passions,
and what not." And thereupon follows that fantastic
utterance concerning the romances of MM. Marivaux
and Crébillon *fils*, which has disconcerted so many of
Gray's admirers. We suspect that any reader who should
nowadays contrast the sickly and sordid intrigue of the
Paysan Parvenu with the healthy animalism of *Joseph
Andrews* would greatly prefer the latter. Yet Gray's
verdict, though cold, is not undiscriminating, and is perhaps as much as one could expect from his cloistered
and fastidious taste.

Various anecdotes, all more or less apocryphal, have
been related respecting the first appearance of *Joseph
Andrews*, and the sum paid to the author for the copyright. A reference to the original assignment, now in
the Forster Library at South Kensington, definitely
settles the latter point. The amount in " lawful Money
of Great Britain," received by " Henry Fielding, Esq."
from "Andrew Millar of St. Clement's Danes in the
Strand," was £183 : 11s. In this document, as in the
order to Nourse of which a *facsimile* is given by Roscoe,
both the author's name and signature are written with
the old-fashioned double f, and he calls himself " Field-

ing " and not " Feilding," like the rest of the Denbigh
family. If we may trust an anecdote given by Kippis,
Lord Denbigh once asked his kinsman the reason of
this difference. " I cannot tell, my lord," returned the
novelist, " unless it be that my branch of the family
was the first that learned to spell."

CHAPTER IV.

THE MISCELLANIES—JONATHAN WILD.

IN March 1742, according to an article in the *Gentleman's Magazine*, attributed to Samuel Johnson, " the most popular Topic of Conversation " was the *Account of the Conduct of the Dowager Dutchess of Marlborough, from her first coming to Court, to the Year* 1710, which, with the help of Hooke of the *Roman History*, the " terrible old Sarah " had just put forth. Among the little cloud of *Sarah-Ads* and *Old Wives' Tales* evoked by this production, was a *Vindication* of her Grace by Fielding, specially prompted, as appears from the title-page, by the " late *scurrilous* Pamphlet" of a " noble Author." If this were not acknowledged to be from Fielding's pen in the Preface to the *Miscellanies* (in which collection, however, it is not reprinted), its authorship would be sufficiently proved by its being included with *Miss Lucy in Town* in the assignment to Andrew Millar referred to at the close of the preceding chapter. The price Millar paid for it was £5 : 5s., or exactly half that of the farce. But it is only reasonable to assume that the Duchess herself (who is said to have given Hooke £5000 for his help) also rewarded her champion. Whether Fielding's

admiration for the "glorious Woman" in whose cause
he had drawn his pen was genuine, or whether—to
use Johnson's convenient euphemism concerning Hooke
—"he was acting only ministerially," are matters for
speculation.   His father, however, had served under the
Duke, and there may have been a traditional attachment
to the Churchills on the part of his family.   It has even
been ingeniously suggested that Sarah Fielding was her
Grace's god-child;[1] but as her mother's name was also
Sarah, no importance can be attached to the suggestion.

Miss Lucy in Town, as its sub-title explains, was a
sequel to the *Virgin Unmask'd*, and was produced at
Drury Lane in May 1742.   As already stated in chapter
ii., Fielding's part in it was small.   It is a lively but
not very creditable trifle, which turns upon certain
equivocal London experiences of the Miss Lucy of
the earlier piece ; and it seems to have been chiefly
intended to afford an opportunity for some clever imitation of the reigning Italian singers by Mrs. Clive and
the famous tenor Beard.   Horace Walpole, who refers to
it in a letter to Mann, between an account of the opening of Ranelagh and an anecdote of Mrs. Bracegirdle,
calls it "a little simple farce," and says that "Mrs. Clive
mimics the Muscovita admirably, and Beard Amorevoli
tolerably."   Mr. Walpole detested the Muscovita, and
adored Amorevoli, which perhaps accounts for the
nice discrimination shown in his praise.   One of the
other characters, Mr. Zorobabel, a Jew, was taken by
Macklin, and from another, Mrs. Haycock (afterwards
changed to Mrs. Midnight), Foote is supposed to have

[1] *Memoirs of Sarah, Duchess of Marlborough*, etc., by Mrs.
A. T. Thomson, 1839.

borrowed Mother Cole in *The Minor*. A third character, Lord Bawble, was considered to reflect upon
"a particular person of quality," and the piece was
speedily forbidden by the Lord Chamberlain, although
it appears to have been acted a few months later
without opposition. One of the results of the prohibi-
tion, according to Mr. Lawrence, was a *Letter to a
Noble Lord* (the Lord Chamberlain) . . . *occasioned by a
Representation . . . of a Farce called " Miss Lucy in Town."*
This, in spite of the Caveat in the Preface to the
Miscellanies, he ascribes to Fielding, and styles it " a
sharp expostulation . . . in which he [Fielding] dis-
avowed any idea of a personal attack."   But Mr.
Lawrence must plainly have been misinformed on the
subject, for the pamphlet bears little sign of Fielding's
hand.   As far as it is intelligible, it is rather against
Miss Lucy than for her, and it makes no reference to
Lord Bawble's original.   The name of this injured
patrician seems indeed never to have transpired; but
he could scarcely have been in any sense a phenomenal
member of the Georgian aristocracy.

In the same month that *Miss Lucy in Town* appeared
at Drury Lane, Millar published it in book form.   In
the following June, T. Waller of the Temple-Cloisters
issued the first of a contemplated series of translations
from Aristophanes by Henry Fielding, Esq., and the
Rev. William Young who sat for Parson Adams.
The play chosen was *Plutus, the God of Riches*, and a
notice upon the original cover stated that, according to
the reception it met with from the public, it would be
followed by the others.   It must be presumed that
" the distressed, and at present, declining State of

Learning" to which the authors referred in their dedication to Lord Talbot, was not a mere form of speech,
for the enterprise does not seem to have met with sufficient encouragement to justify its continuance, and this
special rendering has long since been supplanted by
the more modern versions of Mitchell, Frere, and others.
Whether Fielding took any large share in it is not now
discernible. It is most likely, however, that the bulk
of the work was Young's, and that his colleague did
little more than furnish the Preface, which is partly
written in the first person, and betrays its origin by a
sudden and not very relevant attack upon the "pretty,
dapper, brisk, smart, pert Dialogue" of Modern Comedy
into which the "infinite Wit" of Wycherley had de-
generated under Cibber. It also contains a compliment
to the numbers of the "inimitable Author" of the
Essay on Man.

This is the second compliment which Fielding had
paid to Pope within a brief period, the first having been
that in the *Champion* respecting the translation of the
Iliad. What his exact relations with the author of
the *Dunciad* were, has never been divulged. At first
they seem to have been rather hostile than friendly.
Fielding had ridiculed the Romish Church in the *Old
Debauchees,* a course which Pope could scarcely have
approved ; and he was, moreover, the cousin of Lady
Mary, now no longer throned in the Twickenham
Temple. Pope had commented upon a passage in
Tom Thumb, and Fielding had indirectly referred to
Pope in the *Covent Garden Tragedy.* When it had
been reported that Pope had gone to see *Pasquin,*
the statement had been at once contradicted. But

Fielding was now, like Pope, against Walpole; and *Joseph Andrews* had been published. It may therefore be that the compliments in *Plutus* and the *Champion* were the result of some *rapprochement* between the two. It is, nevertheless, curious that, at this very time, an attempt appears to have been made to connect the novelist with the controversy which presently arose out of Cibber's well-known letter to Pope. In August 1742, the month following its publication, among the pamphlets to which it gave rise, was announced *The Cudgel; or, a Crab-tree Lecture. To the Author of the Dunciad.* "By Hercules Vinegar, Esq." This very mediocre satire in verse is still to be found at the British Museum; but even if it were not included in Fielding's general disclaimer as to unsigned work, it would be difficult to connect it with him. To give but one reason, it would make him the ally and adherent of Cibber,— which is absurd. In all probability, like another Grub Street squib under the same pseudonym, it was by Ralph, who had already attacked Pope, and continued to maintain the Captain's character in the *Champion* long after Fielding had ceased to write for it. It is even possible that Ralph had some share in originating the Vinegar family, for it is noticeable that the paper in which they are first introduced bears no initials. In this case he would consider himself free to adopt the name, however disadvantageous that course might be to Fielding's reputation. And it is clear that, whatever their relations had been in the past, they were for the time on opposite sides in politics, since while Fielding had been vindicating the Duchess of Marlborough, Ralph had been writing against her.

These, however, are minor questions, the discussion of
which would lead too far from the main narrative of
Fielding's life. In the same letter in which Walpole had
referred to *Miss Lucy in Town,* he had spoken of the
success of a new player at Goodman's Fields, after whom
all the town, in Gray's phrase, was "horn-mad;" but
in whose acting Mr. Walpole, with a critical distrust
of novelty, saw nothing particularly wonderful. This
was David Garrick. He had been admitted a student
of Lincoln's Inn a year before Fielding entered the
Middle Temple, had afterwards turned wine-merchant,
and was now delighting London by his versatility in
comedy, tragedy, and farce. One of his earliest theatrical exploits, according to Sir John Hawkins, had been
a private representation of Fielding's *Mock-Doctor,* in a
room over the St. John's Gate, Clerkenwell, so long
familiar to subscribers of the *Gentleman's Magazine ;* his
fellow-actors being Cave's journeymen printers, and
his audience Cave, Johnson, and a few friends. After
this he appears to have made the acquaintance of
Fielding ; and late in 1742, applied to him to know if he
had "any Play by him," as "he was desirous of appear-
ing in a new Part." As a matter of fact Fielding had
two plays by him—the *Good-natured Man* (a title subsequently used by Goldsmith), and a piece called *The
Wedding Day.* The former was almost finished : the latter
was an early work, being indeed "the third Dramatic
Performance he ever attempted." The necessary ar-
rangements having been made with Mr. Fleetwood, the
manager of Drury Lane, Fielding set to work to complete the *Good-natured Man,* which he considered the
better of the two. When he had done so, he came to

the conclusion that it required more attention than he could give it ; and moreover, that the part allotted to Garrick, although it satisfied the actor, was scarcely important enough. He accordingly reverted to the *Wedding Day*, the central character of which had been intended for Wilks. It had many faults which none saw more clearly than the author himself, but he hoped that Garrick's energy and *prestige* would triumphantly surmount all obstacles. He hoped, as well, to improve it by revision. The dangerous illness of his wife, however, made it impossible for him to execute his task; and, as he was pressed for money, the *Wedding Day* was produced on the 17th of February 1743, apparently much as it had been first written some dozen years before. As might be anticipated, it was not a success. The character of Millamour is one which it is hard to believe that even Garrick could have made attractive, and though others of the parts were entrusted to Mrs. Woffington, Mrs. Pritchard, and Macklin, it was acted but six nights. The author's gains were under £50. In the Preface to the *Miscellanies*, from which most of the foregoing account is taken, Fielding, as usual, refers its failure to other causes than its inherent defects. Rumours, he says, had been circulated as to its indecency (and in truth some of the scenes are more than hazardous) ; but it had passed the licenser, and must be supposed to have been up to the moral standard of the time. Its unfavourable reception, as Fielding must have known in his heart, was due to its artistic shortcomings, and also to the fact that a change was taking place in the public taste. It is in connection with the *Wedding Day* that one of the best-known anecdotes of the author is related.

Garrick had begged him to retrench a certain objectionable passage. This Fielding, either from indolence or
unwillingness, declined to do, asserting that if it was
not good, the audience might find it out. The passage
was promptly hissed, and Garrick returned to the green-
room, where the author was solacing himself with a
bottle of champagne. "What is the matter, Garrick?"
said he to the flustered actor; "what are they hissing
now?" He was informed with some heat that they
had been hissing the very scene he had been asked
to withdraw, "and," added Garrick, "they have so
frightened me, that I shall not be able to collect myself
again the whole night."—"Oh!" answered the author,
with an oath, "they HAVE found it out, have they?"
This rejoinder is usually quoted as an instance of Fielding's contempt for the intelligence of his audience; but
nine men in ten, it may be observed, would have said
something of the same sort.

The only other thing which need be referred to in
connection with this comedy—the last of his own
dramatic works which Fielding ever witnessed upon the
stage—is Macklin's doggerel Prologue. Mr. Lawrence
attributes this to Fielding; but he seems to have overlooked the fact that in the *Miscellanies* it is headed,
"*Writ* and Spoken by Mr. Macklin," which gives it more
interest as the work of an outsider than if it had been
a mere laugh by the author at himself. Garrick is represented as too busy to speak the prologue; and Fielding, who has been "drinking to raise his Spirits," has
begged Macklin with his "long, dismal, Mercy-begging
Face," to go on and apologise. Macklin then pretends
to recognise him among the audience, and pokes fun at

his anxieties, telling him that he had better have stuck to "honest *Abram Adams*," who, "in spight of Critics, can make his Readers laugh." The words " in spite of critics " indicate another distinction between Fielding's novels and plays, which should have its weight in any comparison of them. The censors of the pit, in the eighteenth century, seem to have exercised an unusual influence in deciding whether a play should succeed or not ;[1] and, from Fielding's frequent references to friends and enemies, it would almost seem as if he believed their suffrages to be more important than a good plot and a witty dialogue. On the other hand, no coterie of Wits and Templars could kill a book like *Joseph Andrews*. To say nothing of the opportunities afforded by the novel for more leisurely character - drawing, and greater by - play of reflection and description—its reader was an isolated and independent judge ; and in the long run the difference told wonderfully in favour of the author. Macklin was obviously right in recommending Fielding, even in jest, to stick to Parson Adams, and from the familiar publicity of the advice it may also be inferred, not only that the opinion was one commonly current, but that the novel was unusually popular.

The *Wedding Day* was issued separately in February 1743. It must therefore be assumed that the three volumes of· *Miscellanies*, by Henry Fielding, Esq., in which it was reprinted, and to which reference has so often been made in these pages, did not appear until

---

[1] Miller's *Coffee-House*, 1737, for example, was damned by the Templars because it was supposed to reflect on the keepers of " Dick's."—(*Biog. Dramatica.*)

later.[1] They were published by subscription; and
the list, in addition to a large number of aristocratic
and legal names, contains some of more permanent
interest.   Side by side with the Chesterfields and Marl-
boroughs and Burlingtons and Denbighs, come William
Pitt and Henry Fox, Esqs., with Dodington and Winnington and Hanbury Williams.   The theatrical world
is well represented by Garrick and Mrs. Woffington and
Mrs. Clive.   Literature has no names of any eminence
except that of Young; for Savage and Whitehead, Mallet
and Benjamin Hoadly, are certainly *ignes minores*.   Pope
is conspicuous for his absence; so also are Horace Walpole and Gray, while Richardson, of course, is wanting.
Johnson, as yet only the author of *London*, and journey-
man to Cave, could scarcely be expected in the roll; and,
in any case, his friendship for the author of *Pamela* would
probably have kept him away.   Among some other
well‑known eighteenth century names are those of
Dodsley and Millar the booksellers, and the famous
Vauxhall *impresario* Jonathan Tyers.

The first volume of the *Miscellanies*, besides a lengthy
Preface, includes the author's poems, essays *On Conversation*, *On the Knowledge of the Characters of Men*,
On Nothing, a squib upon the transactions of the
Royal Society, a translation from Demosthenes, and
one or two minor pieces.   Much of the biographical
material contained in the Preface has already been made
use of, as well as those verses which can be definitely
dated, or which relate to the author's love‑affairs.
The hitherto unnoticed portions of the volume consist

---

[1] By advertisement in the *London Daily Post and General Advertiser*, they would seem to have been published early in April 1743.

chiefly of Epistles, in the orthodox eighteenth century fashion.   One --- already referred to — is headed
Of True Greatness ; another, inscribed to the Duke of
Richmond, *Of Good-nature ;* while a third is addressed
to a friend *On the Choice of a Wife.* This last contains
some sensible lines, but although Roscoe has managed
to extract two quotable passages, it is needless to imitate
him here.   These productions show no trace of the
authentic Fielding.   The essays are more remarkable,
although, like Montaigne's, they are scarcely described
by their titles.   That on *Conversation* is really a little
treatise on good breeding ; that on the *Characters of
Men,* a lay sermon against Fielding's pet antipathy
—hypocrisy.   Nothing can well be wiser, even now,
than some of the counsels in the former of these
papers on such themes as the limits of raillery, the
duties of hospitality, and the choice of subject in general
conversation.   Nor, however threadbare they may look
to-day, can the final conclusions be reasonably objected
to :—" First, That every Person who indulges his Ill-
nature or Vanity, at the Expense of others ; and in introducing Uneasiness, Vexation, and Confusion into Society,
however exalted or high-titled he may be, is thoroughly
ill-bred ; " and " Secondly, That whoever, from the
Goodness of his Disposition or Understanding, endeavours to his utmost to cultivate the Good-humour and
Happiness of others, and to contribute to the Ease and
Comfort of all his Acquaintance, however low in Rank
Fortune may have placed him, or however clumsy he
may be in his Figure or Demeanour, hath, in the truest
sense of the Word, a Claim to Good-Breeding."   One
fancies that this essay must have been a favourite with

the historian of the *Book of Snobs* and the creator of
Major Dobbin.

The *Characters of Men* is not equal to the *Conversation.*
The theme is a wider one ; and the end proposed,—that
of supplying rules for detecting the real disposition
through all the social disguises which cloak and envelop
it,—can scarcely be said to be attained. But there are
happy touches even in this ; and when the author says
—" I will venture to affirm, that I have known some of
the best sort of Men in the World (to use the vulgar Phrase,)
who would not have scrupled cutting a Friend's Throat ;
and *a Fellow whom no Man should be seen to speak to*, capable
of the highest Acts of Friendship and Benevolence," one
recognises the hand that made the sole good Samaritan
in *Joseph Andrews* "a Lad who hath since been transported
for robbing a Hen-roost." The account of the Terres-
trial Chrysipus or Guinea, a burlesque on a paper read
before the Royal Society on the Fresh Water Polypus,
is chiefly interesting from the fact that it is supposed
to be written by Petrus Gualterus (Peter Walter), who
had an " extraordinary Collection " of them. He died,
in fact, worth £300,000. The only other paper in the
volume of any value is a short one *Of the Remedy of
Affliction for the Loss of our Friends,* to which we shall
presently return.

The farce of *Eurydice,* and the *Wedding Day,* which,
with *A Journey from this World to the Next,* etc., make up
the contents of the second volume of the *Miscellanies,*
have been already sufficiently discussed. But the *Journey*
deserves some further notice. It has been suggested
that this curious Lucianic production may have been
prompted by the vision of Mercury and Charon in the

Champion, though the kind of allegory of which it consists is common enough with the elder essayists ; and it
is notable that another book was published in April 1743,
under the title of *Cardinal Fleury's Journey to the other
World*, which is manifestly suggested by Quevedo.
Fielding's *Journey*, however, is a fragment which the
author feigns to have found in the garret of a stationer
in the Strand.   Sixteen out of five-and-twenty chapters in
Book i. are occupied with the transmigrations of Julian
the Apostate, which are not concluded.   Then follows
another chapter from Book xix., which contains the history of Anna Boleyn, and the whole breaks off abruptly.
Its best portion is undoubtedly the first ten chapters,
which relate the writer's progress to Elysium, and afford
opportunity for many strokes of satire.   Such are the
whimsical terror of the spiritual traveller in the stage-
coach, who hears suddenly that his neighbour has died
of smallpox, a disease he had been dreading all his life ;
and the punishment of Lord Scrape, the miser, who is
doomed to dole out money to all comers, and who, after
"being purified in the Body of a Hog," is ultimately to
return to earth again.   Nor is the delight of some of
those who profit by his enforced assistance less keenly
realised :—" I remarked a poetical Spirit in particular,
who swore he would have a hearty Gripe at him : 'For,
says he, the Rascal not only refused to subscribe to my
Works ; but sent back my Letter unanswered, tho' I'm
a better Gentleman than himself.'"   The descriptions of
the City of Diseases, the Palace of Death, and the Wheel
of Fortune from which men draw their chequered lots,
are all unrivalled in their way.   But here, as always, it
is in his pictures of human nature that Fielding shines,

and it is this that makes the chapters in which Minos
is shown adjudicating upon the separate claims of the
claimants to enter Elysium the most piquant of all.
The virtuoso and butterfly hunter, who is repulsed " with
great Scorn ;" the dramatic author who is admitted (to
his disgust), not on account of his works, but because he
has once lent " the whole Profits of a Benefit Night to a
Friend ;" the parson who is turned back, while his poor
parishioners are admitted ; and the trembling wretch
who has been hanged for a robbery of eighteen-pence, to
which he had been driven by poverty, but whom the judge
welcomes cordially because he had been a kind father,
husband, and son; all these are conceived in that humane
and generous spirit which is Fielding's most engaging
characteristic.   The chapter immediately following, which
describes the literary and other inhabitants of Elysium,
is even better.   Here is Leonidas, who appears to be
only moderately gratified with the honour recently done
him by Mr. Glover the poet ; here is Homer, toying with
Madam Dacier, and profoundly indifferent as to his birthplace and the continuity of his poems ; here, too, is Shakespeare, who, foreseeing future commentators and the "New
Shakespere Society," declines to enlighten Betterton and
Booth as to a disputed passage in his works, adding, " I
marvel nothing so much as that Men will gird themselves
at discovering obscure Beauties in an Author.   Certes
the greatest and most pregnant Beauties are ever the
plainest and most evidently striking ; and when two
Meanings of a Passage can in the least ballance our Judge-
ments which to prefer, I hold it matter of unquestionable
Certainty that neither is worth a farthing."   Then, again,
there are Addison and Steele, who are described with so

pleasant a knowledge of their personalities that, although
the passage has been often quoted, there seems to be no
reason why it should not be quoted once more :—

" *Virgil* then came up to me, with Mr. *Addison* under his
Arm. Well, Sir, said he, how many Translations have these
few last Years produced of my *Æneid ?* I told him, I believed
several, but I could not possibly remember ; for I had never
read any but Dr. *Trapp's.*[1]—Ay, said he, that is a curious
Piece indeed ! I then acquainted him with the Discovery
made by Mr. *Warburton* of the *Eleusinian* Mysteries couched
in his 6th book. What Mysteries ? said Mr. *Addison.* The
Eleusinian, answered *Virgil,* which I have disclosed in my
6th Book. How ! replied *Addison.* You never mentioned
a word of any such Mysteries to me in all our Acquaintance.
I thought it was unnecessary, cried the other, to a Man of
your infinite Learning : besides, you always told me, you
perfectly understood my meaning. Upon this I thought the
Critic looked a little out of countenance, and turned aside
to a very merry Spirit, one *Dick Steele,* who embraced him,
and told him, He had been the greatest Man upon Earth ;
that he readily resigned up all the Merit of his own Works
to him. Upon which, *Addison* gave him a gracious Smile,
and clapping him on the Back with much Solemnity, cried
out, *Well said, Dick.*"

After encountering these and other notabilities, including Tom Thumb and Livy, the latter of whom takes
occasion to commend the ingenious performances of Lady
Marlborough's assistant, Mr. Hooke, the author meets
with Julian the Apostate, and from this point the narrative grows languid. Its unfinished condition may perhaps be accepted as a proof that Fielding himself had
wearied of his scheme.

The third volume of the *Miscellanies* is wholly occupied with the remarkable work entitled the *History of the
Life of the late Mr. Jonathan Wild the Great.* As in the

[1] Dr. Trapp's translation of the *Æneid* was published in 1718.

case of the *Journey from this World to the Next*, it is not
unlikely that the first germ of this may be found in
the pages of the *Champion*. "Reputation"—says Fielding in one of the essays in that periodical—"often
courts those most who regard her the least. Actions
have sometimes been attended with Fame, which were
undertaken in Defiance of it. *Jonathan Wyld* himself
had for many years no small Share of it in this Kingdom." The book now under consideration is the elaboration of the idea thus casually thrown out. Under
the name of a notorious thief-taker hanged at Tyburn
in 1725, Fielding has traced the Progress of a Rogue
to the Gallows, showing by innumerable subtle touches
that the (so-called) greatness of a villain does not
very materially differ from any other kind of greatness, which is equally independent of goodness. This
continually suggested affinity between the ignoble and
the pseudo-noble is the text of the book. Against
genuine worth (its author is careful to explain) his satire
is in no wise directed. He is far from considering
"*Newgate* as no other than Human Nature with its
Mask off;" but he thinks "we may be excused for sus-
pecting, that the splendid Palaces of the Great are often
no other than *Newgate* with the Mask on." Thus *Jonathan Wild the Great* is a prolonged satire upon the spurious eminence in which benevolence, honesty, charity,
and the like have no part; or, as Fielding prefers to
term it, that false or "Bombast greatness" which is so
often mistaken for the "*true Sublime* in Human Nature"
—Greatness and Goodness combined. So thoroughly
has he explained his intention in the Prefaces to the
Miscellanies, and to the book itself, that it is difficult to

comprehend how Scott could fail to see his drift. Possibly, like some others, he found the subject repugnant
and painful to his kindly nature. Possibly, too, he did
not, for this reason, study the book very carefully, for,
with the episode of Heartfree under one's eyes, it is
not strictly accurate to say (as he does) that it presents
"a picture of complete vice, *unrelieved by any thing of
human feeling*, and never by any accident even deviating
into virtue." If the author's introduction be borne in
mind, and if the book be read steadily in the light there
supplied, no one can refrain from admiring the extraordinary skill and concentration with which the plan is
pursued, and the adroitness with which, at every turn,
the villainy of Wild is approximated to that of those
securer and more illustrious criminals with whom he is
so seldom confused. And Fielding has never carried
one of his chief and characteristic excellences to so great
perfection : the book is a model of sustained and sleep-
less irony. To make any extracts from it—still less to
make any extracts which should do justice to it, is almost
impracticable ; but the edifying discourse between Wild
and Count La Ruse in Book i., and the pure comedy of
that in Book iv. with the Ordinary of Newgate (who objects to wine, but drinks punch because "it is no where
spoken against in Scripture "), as well as the account of
the prison faction between Wild and Johnson,[1] with its

[1] Some critics at this point appear to have identified Johnson
and Wild with Lord Wilmington and Sir Robert Walpole (who resigned in 1742), while Mr. Keightley suspects that Wild throughout typifies Walpole. But, in his advertisement to the edition of
1754, Fielding expressly disclaims any such "personal Application."
"The Truth is (he says), as a very corrupt State of Morals is here
represented, the Scene seems very properly to have been laid in

admirable speech of the "grave Man" against Party, may
all be cited as examples of its style and method.   Nor
should the character of Wild in the last chapter, and
his famous rules of conduct, be neglected.   It must be
admitted, however, that the book is not calculated to
suit the nicely-sensitive in letters; or, it may be added,
those readers for whom the evolution of a purely intellectual conception is either unmeaning or uninteresting.
Its place in Fielding's works is immediately after his
three great novels, and this is more by reason of its
subject than its workmanship, which could hardly be
excelled.   When it was actually composed is doubtful.
If it may be connected with the already-quoted passage
in the *Champion*, it must be placed after March 1740,
which is the date of the paper; but, from a reference to
Peter Pounce in Book ii., it might also be supposed
to have been written after *Joseph Andrews*.   The Bath
simile in chapter xiv. Book i., makes it likely that some
part of it was penned at that place, where, from an epi-
gram in the *Miscellanies* "written *Extempore* in the Pump
Room," it is clear that Fielding was staying in 1742.
But, whenever it was completed, we are inclined to think
that it was planned and begun before *Joseph Andrews*
was published, as it is in the highest degree improbable
that Fielding, always carefully watching the public taste,
would have followed up that fortunate adventure in a
new direction by a work so entirely different from it as
Jonathan Wild.

Newgate: Nor do I see any Reason for introducing any allegory
at all; unless we will agree that there are, without those Walls,
some other Bodies of Men of worse Morals than those within; and
who have, consequently, a Right to change Places with its present
Inhabitants."

A second edition of the *Miscellanies* appeared in the same year as the first, namely in 1743. From this date until the publication of *Tom Jones* in 1749, Fielding produced no work of signal importance, and his personal history for the next few years is exceedingly obscure. We are inclined to suspect that this must have been the most trying period of his career. His health was shattered, and he had become a martyr to gout, which seriously interfered with the active practice of his profession. Again, "about this time," says Murphy vaguely, after speaking of the *Wedding Day*, he lost his first wife. That she was alive in the winter of 1742-3 is clear, for, in the Preface to the *Miscellanies*, he describes himself as being then laid up, "with a favourite Child dying in one Bed, and my Wife in a Condition very little better, on another, attended with other Circumstances, which served as very proper Decorations to such a Scene,"—by which Mr. Keightley no doubt rightly supposes him to refer to writs and bailiffs. It must also be assumed that Mrs. Fielding was alive when the Preface was written, since, in apologising for an apparent delay in publishing the book, he says the "real Reason" was "the dangerous Illness of one from whom I *draw* [the italics are ours] all the solid Comfort of my Life." There is another unmistakable reference to her in one of the minor papers in the first volume, viz. that *Of the Remedy of Affliction for the Loss of our Friends.* "I remember the most excellent of Women, and tenderest of Mothers, when, after a painful and dangerous Delivery, she was told she had a Daughter, answering; *Good God! have I produced a Creature who is to undergo what I have suffered!* Some Years afterwards, I heard the same Woman, on the

Death of that very Child, then one of the loveliest Creatures ever seen, comforting herself with reflecting, that
*her Child could never know what it was to feel such a Loss as
she then lamented.*" Were it not for the passages already
quoted from the Preface, it might almost be concluded
from the tone of the foregoing quotation and the final
words of the paper, which refer to our meeting with those
we have lost in Heaven, that Mrs. Fielding was already
dead. But the use of the word "draw" in the Preface affords distinct evidence to the contrary. It is
therefore most probable that she died in the latter part
of 1743, having been long in a declining state of health.
For a time her husband was inconsolable. "The fortitude of mind," says Murphy, "with which he met all the
other calamities of life, deserted him on this most trying
occasion." His grief was so vehement "that his friends
began to think him in danger of losing his reason."

That Fielding had depicted his first wife in Sophia
Western has already been pointed out, and we have
the authority of Lady Mary Wortley Montagu and
Richardson for saying that she was afterwards reproduced in *Amelia.* "Amelia," says the latter, in a letter
to Mrs. Donnellan, "even to her *noselessness,* is again his
first wife." Some of her traits, too, are to be detected in
the Mrs. Wilson of *Joseph Andrews.* But, beyond these
indications, we hear little about her. Almost all that
is definitely known is contained in a passage of the
admirable *Introductory Anecdotes* contributed by Lady
Louisa Stuart in 1837 to Lord Wharncliffe's edition of
Lady Mary Wortley Montagu's *Letters and Works.* This
account was based upon the recollections of Lady Bute,
Lady Mary's daughter.

"Only those persons (says Lady Stuart) are mentioned
here of whom Lady Bute could speak from her own recollec-
tion or her mother's report. Both had made her well informed of every particular that concerned her relation Henry
Fielding ; nor was she a stranger to that beloved first wife
whose picture he drew in his Amelia, where, as she said, even
the glowing language he knew how to employ did not do
more than justice to the amiable qualities of the original, or
to her beauty, although this had suffered a little from the
accident related in the novel,—a frightful overturn, which
destroyed the gristle of her nose.[1] He loved her passionately,
and she returned his affection ; yet led no happy life, for they
were almost always miserably poor, and seldom in a state of
quiet and safety. All the world knows what was his imprudence ; if ever he possessed a score of pounds, nothing could
keep him from lavishing it idly, or make him think of to-
morrow. Sometimes they were living in decent lodgings
with tolerable comfort; sometimes in a wretched garret without necessaries ; not to speak of the spunging-houses and
hiding-places where he was occasionally to be found. His

[1] That any one could have remained lovely after such a
catastrophe is difficult to believe. But probably Lady Bute (or
Lady Stuart) exaggerated its effects ; for—to say nothing of the
fact that, throughout the novel, Amelia's beauty is continually
commended—in the delightfully feminine description which is
given of her by Mrs. James in Book xi. chap. i., pp. 114-15 of the
first edition of 1752, although she is literally pulled to pieces, there
is no reference whatever to her nose, which may be taken as proof
positive that it was not an assailable feature. Moreover, in the book
as we now have it, Fielding, obviously in deference to contemporary
criticism, inserted the following specific passages :—"She was,
indeed, a most charming woman ; and I know not whether the
little scar on her nose did not rather add to, than diminish her
beauty" (Book iv. chap. vii.); and in Mrs. James's portrait :—
"Then her nose, as well proportioned as it is, has a visible scar on
one side." No previous biographer seems to have thought it necessary to make any mention of these statements, while Johnson's
speech about "That vile broken nose, *never cured,*" and Richardson's coarsely-malignant utterance to Mrs. Donnellan, are everywhere industriously remembered and repeated.

elastic gaiety of spirit carried him through it all ; but, meanwhile, care and anxiety were preying upon her more delicate
mind, and undermining her constitution.   She gradually
declined, caught a fever, and died in his arms."

As usual, Mr. Keightley has done his best to test this
statement to the utmost.   Part of his examination may
be neglected, because it is based upon the misconception that Lord Wharncliffe, Lady Mary's greatgrand-
son, and not Lady Stuart, her granddaughter, was the
writer of the foregoing account.   But as a set-off to
the extreme destitution alleged, Mr. Keightley very
justly observes that Mrs. Fielding must for some time
have had a maid, since it was a maid who had been
devotedly attached to her whom Fielding subsequently
married.   He also argues that "living in a garret and
skulking in out o' the way retreats," are incompatible
with studying law and practising as a barrister.   Making every allowance, however, for the somewhat exaggerated way in which those of high rank often speak of
the distresses of their less opulent kinsfolk, it is probable that Fielding's married life was one of continual
shifts and privations.   Such a state of things is completely in accordance with his profuse nature [1] and his
precarious means.   Of his family by the first Mrs. Fielding no very material particulars have been preserved.
Writing, in November 1745, in the *True Patriot*, he
speaks of having a son and a daughter, but no son
by his first wife seems to have survived him.   The
late Colonel Chester found the burial of a "James
Fielding, son of Henry Fielding," recorded under date
of 19th February 1736, in the register of St. Giles in

---

[1] The passage as to his imprudence is, oddly enough, omitted
from Mr. Keightley's quotation.

the Fields ; but it is by no means certain that this entry refers to the novelist. A daughter, Eleanor Harriot, certainly did survive him, for she is mentioned in the *Voyage to Lisbon* as being of the party who accompanied him. Another daughter, as already stated, probably died in the winter of 1742-3 ; and the *Journey from this World to the Next* contains the touching reference to this or another child, of which Dickens writes so warmly in one of his letters. " I presently," says Fielding, speaking of his entrance into Elysium, "met a little Daughter, whom I had lost several Years before. Good Gods ! what Words can describe the Raptures, the melting passionate Tenderness, with which we kiss'd each other, continuing in our Embrace, with the most extatic Joy, a Space, which if Time had been measured here as on Earth, could not have been less than half a Year."

From the death of Mrs. Fielding until the publication of the *True Patriot* in 1745 another comparative blank ensues in Fielding's history ; and it can only be filled by the assumption that he was still endeavouring to follow his profession as a barrister. His literary work seems to have been confined to a Preface to the second edition of his sister's novel of *David Simple*, which appeared in 1744. This, while rendering fraternal justice to that now forgotten book, is memorable for some personal utterances on Fielding's part. In denying the authorship of *David Simple*, which had been attributed to him, he takes occasion to appeal against the injustice of referring anonymous works to his pen, in the face of his distinct engagement in the Preface to the *Miscellanies*, that he would thenceforth write nothing except over his own signature ; and he complains that such a course has a tendency to injure him in a profession to which "he has applied with so arduous and intent a diligence, that he has had no leisure, if he had inclination, to compose anything of this kind (i.e. *David Simple*)." At the same time, he formally withdraws his promise, since it has in no wise exempted him from the scandal of putting forth anonymous work. From other passages in this "Preface," it may be gathered the immediate cause of irritation was the assignment to his pen of "that infamous paultry libel" the *Causidicade*, a satire directed at the law in general, and some of the subscribers to the *Miscellanies* in particular. "This," he says, "accused me not only of being a bad writer, and a bad man, but with downright idiotism, in flying in the face of the greatest men of my profession." It may easily be conceived that such a report must be unfavourable to a struggling barrister, and Fielding's anxiety on this head is a strong proof that he was still hoping to succeed at the Bar. To a subsequent collection of *Familiar Letters between the Principal Characters in David Simple and some others*, he supplied another preface three years later; but beyond a complimentary reference to Lyttelton's *Persian Letters*, it has no biographical interest.

A life of ups and downs like Fielding's is seldom remarkable for its consistency. It is therefore not surprising to find that, despite his desire in 1744 to refrain from writing, he was again writing in 1745. The landing of Charles Edward attracted him once more into the ranks of journalism, on the side of the Government, and gave rise to the *True Patriot*, a weekly paper, the first number of which appeared in November. This, having come to an end with the

Rebellion, was succeeded in December 1747 by the
Jacobite's Journal, supposed to emanate from "John
Trott-Plaid, Esq.," and intended to push the discomfit-
ure of Jacobite sentiment still further. It is needless
to discuss these mainly political efforts at any length.
They are said to have been highly approved by those in
power : it is certain that they earned for their author the
stigma of "pension'd scribbler." Both are now very
rare ; and in Murphy the former is represented by
twenty-four numbers, the latter by two only. The *True
Patriot* contains a dream of London abandoned to the
rebels, which is admirably graphic ; and there is also a
prophetic chronicle of events for 1746, in which the
same idea is treated in a lighter and more satirical vein.
But perhaps the most interesting feature is the reappear-
ance of Parson Adams, who addresses a couple of
letters to the same periodical—one on the rising generally, and the other on the "young England" of the
day, as exemplified in a very offensive specimen he
had recently encountered at Mr. Wilson's. Other
minor points of interest in connection with the
Jacobite's Journal, are the tradition associating Hogarth
with the rude woodcut headpiece (a Scotch man and
woman on an ass led by a monk) which surmounted its
earlier numbers, and the genial welcome given in No. 5,
perhaps not without some touch of contrition, to the
two first volumes, then just published, of Richardson's
Clarissa. The pen is the pen of an imaginary "correspondent," but the words are unmistakably Fielding's :—

"When I tell you I have lately received this Pleasure [*i.e.*
of reading a new master-piece], you will not want me to
inform you that I owe it to the Author of CLARISSA. Such

I

Simplicity, such Manners, such deep Penetration into Nature;
such Power to raise and alarm the Passions, few Writers,
either ancient or modern, have been possessed of.   My Affections are so strongly engaged, and my Fears are so raised, by
what I have already read, that I cannot express my Eagerness
to see the rest.   Sure this Mr. *Richardson* is Master of all
that Art which *Horace* compares to Witchcraft
                    —Pectus inaniter angit,
              Irritat, mulcet, falsis terroribus implet
              Ut Magus.—"

Between the discontinuance of the *True Patriot* and
the establishment of its successor occurred an event, the
precise date of which has been hitherto unknown, namely,
Fielding's second marriage.   The account given of this
by Lady Louisa Stuart is as follows :—

" His [Fielding's] biographers seem to have been shy of
disclosing that after the death of this charming woman [his
first wife] he married her maid.   And yet the act was not
so discreditable to his character as it may sound.   The maid
had few personal charms, but was an excellent creature, devotedly attached to her mistress, and almost broken-hearted
for her loss.   In the first agonies of his own grief, which approached to frenzy, he found no relief but from weeping along
with her ; nor solace, when a degree calmer, but in talking
to her of the angel they mutually regretted.   This made her
his habitual confidential associate, and in process of time he
began to think he could not give his children a tenderer
mother, or secure for himself a more faithful housekeeper and
nurse.   At least this was what he told his friends ; and it is
certain that her conduct as his wife confirmed it, and fully
justified his good opinion."

It has now been ascertained that the marriage took
place at St. Bene't's, Paul's Wharf, an obscure little church
in the City, at present surrendered to a Welsh congrega-
tion, but at that time, like Mary-le-bone old church, much

in request for unions of a private character. The date
in the register is the 27th of November 1747. The
second Mrs. Fielding's maiden name, which has been
hitherto variously reported as Macdonnell, Macdonald,
and Macdaniel, is given as Mary Daniel,[1] and she is further
described as "of St. Clement's Danes, Middlesex, Spin-
ster." Either previously to this occurrence, or immediately after it, Fielding seems to have taken two rooms in
a house in Back Lane, Twickenham, "not far," says the
Rev. Mr. Cobbett in his *Memorials*, "from the site of
Copt Hall." In 1872 this house was still standing,—a
quaint old-fashioned wooden structure;[2]—and from hence,
on the 25th February 1748, was baptized the first of the
novelist's sons concerning whom any definite information exists—the William Fielding who, like his father,
became a Westminster magistrate. Beyond suggesting
that it may supply a reason why, during Mrs. Fielding's
life-time, her husband's earliest biographer made no reference to the marriage, it is needless to dwell upon the
proximity between the foregoing dates. In other respects
the circumstance now first made public is not inconsistent
with Lady Stuart's narrative; and there is no doubt,
from the references to her in the *Journal of a Voyage to
Lisbon* and elsewhere, that Mary Daniel did prove an
excellent wife, mother, and nurse. Another thing is
made clear by the date established, and this is that
the verses "On Felix; Marry'd to a Cook-Maid" in the
Gentleman's Magazine for July 1746, to which Mr. Lawrence
refers, cannot possibly have anything to do with Fielding,

---

[1] See note to Fielding's letter in Chap. vii.
[2] Now (1883) it no longer exists, and a row of cottages occupies
the site.

although they seem to indicate that alliances of the kind were not unusual. Perhaps *Pamela* had made them fashionable. On the other hand, the supposed allusion to Lyttelton and Fielding, to be found in the first edition of *Peregrine Pickle*, but afterwards suppressed, receives a certain confirmation. " When," says Smollett, speaking of the relations of an imaginary Mr. Spondy with Gosling Scrag, who is understood to represent Lyttelton, " he is inclined to marry his own cook-wench, his gracious patron may condescend to give the bride away ; and may finally settle him in his old age, as a trading Westminster justice." That, looking to the facts, Fielding's second marriage should have gained the approval and countenance of Lyttelton is no more than the upright and honourable character of the latter would lead us to expect.

The *Jacobite's Journal* ceased to appear in November 1748. In the early part of the December following, the remainder of Smollett's programme came to pass, and by Lyttelton's interest Fielding was appointed a Justice of the Peace for Westminster. From a letter in the *Bedford Correspondence*, dated 13th December 1748, respecting the lease of a house or houses which would qualify him to act for Middlesex, it would seem that the county was afterwards added to his commission. He must have entered upon his office in the first weeks of December, as upon the ninth of that month one John Salter was committed to the Gatehouse by Henry Fielding, Esq., " of Bow Street, Covent Garden, formerly Sir Thomas de Veil's." Sir Thomas de Veil, who died in 1746, and whose *Memoirs* had just been published, could not, however, have been Fielding's immediate predecessor.

CHAPTER V.

TOM JONES.

WRITING from Basingstoke to his brother Tom, on the 29th October 1746, Joseph Warton thus refers to a visit he paid to Fielding :—

"I wish you had been with me last week, when I spent two evenings with Fielding and his sister, who wrote David Simple, and you may guess I was very well entertained. The lady indeed retir'd pretty soon, but Russell and I sat up with the Poet [Warton no doubt uses the word here in the sense of 'maker' or 'creator'] till one or two in the morning, and were inexpressibly diverted. I find he values, as he justly may, his Joseph Andrews above all his writings : he was extremely civil to me, I fancy, on my Father's account." [1]

This mention of *Joseph Andrews* has misled some of Fielding's biographers into thinking that he ranked that novel above *Tom Jones*. But, in October 1746, *Tom Jones* had not been published ; and, from the absence of any reference to it by Warton, it is only reasonable to conclude that it had not yet assumed a definite form, or Fielding, who was by no means uncommunicative, would in all probability have spoken of it

---

[1] *i.e.* the Rev. Thomas Warton, Vicar of Basingstoke, and sometime Professor of Poetry at Oxford.

as an effort from which he expected still greater things.
It is clear, too, that at this date he was staying in London,
presumably in lodgings with his sister; and it is also
most likely that he lived much in town when he was conducting the *True Patriot* and the *Jacobite's Journal*. At
other times he would appear to have had no settled place
of abode. There are traditions that *Tom Jones* was composed in part at Salisbury, in a house at the foot of
Milford Hill; and again that it was written at Twiverton,
or Twerton-on-Avon, near Bath, where, as the Vicar
pointed out in *Notes and Queries* for March 15th, 1879,
there still exists a house called Fielding's Lodge, over
the door of which is a stone crest of a phœnix rising out
of a mural coronet. This latter tradition is supported
by the statement of Mr. Richard Graves, author of the
Spiritual Quixote, and rector, *circa* 1750, of the neighbouring parish of Claverton, who says in his *Trifling
Anecdotes of the late Ralph Allen*, that Fielding while at
Twerton used to dine almost daily with Allen at Prior
Park. There are also traces of his residence at Bath
itself; and of visits to the seat of Lyttelton's father at
Hagley in Worcestershire. Towards the close of 1747
he had, as before stated, rooms in Back Lane, Twickenham; and it must be to this or to some earlier period
that Walpole alludes in his *Parish Register* (1759):—

> "Here Fielding met his bunter Muse
> And, as they quaff'd the fiery juice,
> Droll Nature stamp'd each lucky hit
> With unimaginable wit;"—

a quatrain in which the last lines excuse the first. According to Mr. Cobbett's already-quoted *Memorials of
Twickenham*, he left that place upon his appointment as a

Middlesex magistrate, when he moved to Bow Street. His house in Bow Street belonged to John, Duke of Bedford; and he continued to live in it until a short time before his death. It was subsequently occupied by his half-brother and successor, Sir John,[1] who, writing to the Duke in March 1770, to thank him for his munificent gift of an additional ten years to the lease, recalls "that princely instance of generosity which his Grace shewed to his late brother, Henry Fielding."

What this was, is not specified. It may have been the gift of the leases of those tenements which, as explained, were necessary to qualify Fielding to act as a Justice of the Peace for the county of Middlesex; it may even have been the lease of the Bow Street house; or it may have been simply a gift of money. But whatever it was, it was something considerable. In his appeal to the Duke, at the close of the last chapter, Fielding referred to previous obligations, and in his dedication of *Tom Jones* to Lyttelton, he returns again to his Grace's beneficence. Another person, of whose kindness grateful but indirect mention is made in the same dedication, is Ralph Allen, who, according to Derrick, the Bath M.C., sent the novelist a present of £200, before he had even made his acquaintance,[2] which, from the reference to Allen in *Joseph Andrews*, probably began before 1743. Lastly, there is Lyttelton himself, concerning whom, in addition to a sentence which implies that he actually suggested the writing of *Tom Jones*, we have

[1] In the riots of '80—as Dickens has not forgotten to note in *Barnaby Rudge*—the house was destroyed by the mob, who burned Sir John's goods in the street (Boswell's *Johnson*, chap. lxx.)

[2] Derrick's *Letters*, 1767, ii. 95.

the express statements on Fielding's part that "without
your Assistance this History had never been completed,"
and "I partly owe to you my Existence during great
Part of the Time which I have employed in composing
it." These words must plainly be accepted as indicating
pecuniary help ; and, taking all things together, there
can be little doubt that for some years antecedent to his
appointment as a Justice of the Peace, Fielding was in
straitened circumstances, and was largely aided, if not
practically supported, by his friends. Even supposing
him to have been subsidised by Government as alleged,
his profits from the *True Patriot* and the *Jacobite's Journal*
could not have been excessive ; and his gout, of which
he speaks in one of his letters to the Duke of Bedford,
must have been a serious obstacle in the way of his legal
labours.

The History of Tom Jones, a Foundling, was published
by Andrew Millar on the 28th of February 1749, and
its appearance in six volumes, 12mo, was announced in
the *General Advertizer* of that day's date. There had been
no author's name on the title-page of *Joseph Andrews ;*
but *Tom Jones* was duly described as "by Henry Fielding,
Esq.," and bore the motto from Horace, seldom so justly
applied, of "*Mores hominum multorum vidit.*" The advertisement also ingenuously stated that as it was "impossible
to get Sets bound fast enough to answer the Demand for
them, such Gentlemen and Ladies as pleased, might have
them sew'd in Blue Paper and Boards at the Price of
16s. a Set." The date of issue sufficiently disposes of
the statement of Cunningham and others, that the book
was written at Bow Street. Little more than the
dedication, which is preface as well, can have been pro-

duced by Fielding in his new home. Making fair allowance for the usual tardy progress of a book through the
press, and taking into consideration the fact that the
author was actively occupied with his yet unfamiliar
magisterial duties, it is most probable that the last chapter
of *Tom Jones* had been penned before the end of 1748,
and that after that time it had been at the printer's. For
the exact price paid to the author by the publisher on
this occasion we are indebted to Horace Walpole, who,
writing to George Montagu in May 1749, says—" Millar
the bookseller has done very generously by him [Field-
ing] : finding Tom Jones, for which he had given him
six hundred pounds, sell so greatly, he has since given
him another hundred."

It is time, however, to turn from these particulars to
the book itself. In *Joseph Andrews*, Fielding's work had
been mainly experimental. He had set out with an
intention which had unexpectedly developed into something else. That something else, he had explained, was
the comic epic in prose. He had discovered its scope
and possibilities only when it was too late to re-cast his
original design ; and though *Joseph Andrews* has all the
freshness and energy of a first attempt in a new direction, it has also the manifest disadvantages of a mixed
conception and an uncertain plan. No one had per-
ceived these defects more plainly than the author ; and
in *Tom Jones* he set himself diligently to perfect his
new-found method. He believed that he foresaw a
"new Province of Writing," of which he regarded himself with justice as the founder and lawgiver ; and in the
"prolegomenous, or introductory Chapters " to each book
—those delightful resting-spaces where, as George Eliot

says, "he seems to bring his arm-chair to the proscenium
and chat with us in all the lusty ease of his fine English"
—he takes us, as it were, into his confidence, and discourses frankly of his aims and his way of work.   He
looked upon these little "initial Essays" indeed, as an
indispensable part of his scheme.   They have given him,
says he more than once, "the greatest Pains in composing"
of any part of his book, and he hopes that, like the
Greek and Latin mottoes in the *Spectator*, they may serve
to secure him against imitation by inferior writers.[1]
Naturally a great deal they contain is by this time
commonplace, although it was unhackneyed enough when
Fielding wrote.   The absolute necessity in writing of this
kind for genius, learning, and knowledge of the world,
the constant obligation to preserve character and probability—to regard variety and the law of contrast :—
these are things with which the modern tiro (however
much he may fail to possess or observe them) is now
supposed to be at least theoretically acquainted.   But
there are other chapters in which Fielding may also
be said to reveal his personal point of view, and
these can scarcely be disregarded.   His "Fare," he
says, following the language of the table, is "HÚMAN
NATURE," which he shall first present "in that more
plain and simple Manner in which it is found in the
Country," and afterwards "hash and ragoo it with all
the high *French* and *Italian* seasoning of Affectation and
Vice which Courts and Cities afford."   His inclination,

---

[1] Notwithstanding this warning, Cumberland (who copied so
much) copied these in his novel of *Henry*.   On the other hand,
Fielding's French and Polish translators omitted them as superfluous.

he admits, is rather to the middle and lower classes than to "the highest Life," which he considers to present "very little Humour or Entertainment." His characters (as before) are based upon actual experience ; or, as he terms it, "Conversation." He does not propose to present his reader with "Models of Perfection;" he has never happened to meet with those "faultless Monsters." He holds that mankind is constitutionally defective, and that a single bad act does not, of necessity, imply a bad nature. He has also observed, without surprise, that virtue in this world is not always "the certain Road to Happiness," nor "Vice to Misery." In short, having been admitted "behind the Scenes of this Great Theatre of Nature," he paints humanity as he has found it, extenuating nothing, nor setting down aught in malice, but reserving the full force of his satire and irony for affectation and hypocrisy. His sincere endeavour, he says moreover in his dedication to Lyttelton, has been "to recommend Goodness and Innocence," and promote the cause of religion and virtue. And he has all the consciousness that what he is engaged upon is no ordinary enterprise. He is certain that his pages will outlive both "their own infirm Author" and his enemies ; and he appeals to Fame to solace and reassure him—

"Come, bright Love of Fame,"—says the beautiful "Invocation" which begins the thirteenth Book,—"inspire my glowing Breast : Not thee I call, who over swelling Tides of Blood and Tears, dost bear the Heroe on to Glory, while Sighs of Millions waft his spreading Sails ; but thee, fair, gentle Maid, whom *Mnesis*, happy Nymph, first on the Banks of *Hebrus* didst produce. Thee, whom *Maeonia* educated, whom *Mantua* charm'd, and who, on that fair Hill which overlooks the proud Metropolis of *Britain*, sat, with thy *Milton*, sweetly

tuning the Heroic Lyre; fill my ravished Fancy with the
Hopes of charming Ages yet to come. Foretel me that some
tender Maid, whose Grandmother is yet unborn, hereafter,
when, under the fictitious Name of *Sophia*, she reads the real
Worth which once existed in my *Charlotte*, shall, from her
sympathetic Breast, send forth the heaving Sigh. Do thou
teach me not only to foresee, but to enjoy, nay, even to feed
on future Praise. Comfort me by a solemn Assurance, that
when the little Parlour in which I sit at this Instant, shall
be reduced to a worse furnished Box, I shall be read, with
Honour, by those who never knew nor saw me, and whom I
shall neither know nor see."

With no less earnestness, after a mock apostrophe to
Wealth, he appeals to Genius :—

" Teach me (he exclaims), which to thee is no difficult
Task, to know Mankind better than they know themselves.
Remove that Mist which dims the Intellects of Mortals, and
causes them to adore Men for their Art, or to detest them
for their Cunning in deceiving others, when they are, in
Reality, the Objects only of Ridicule, for deceiving themselves.
Strip off the thin Disguise of Wisdom from Self-Conceit, of
Plenty from Avarice, and of Glory from Ambition. Come
thou, that hast inspired thy *Aristophanes*, thy *Lucian*, thy
Cervantes, thy *Rabelais*, thy *Molière*, thy *Shakespear*, thy *Swift*,
thy *Marivaux*, fill my Pages with Humour, 'till Mankind
learn the Good-Nature to laugh only at the Follies of others,
and the Humility to grieve at their own."

From the little group of immortals who are here
enumerated, it may be gathered with whom Fielding
sought to compete, and with whom he hoped hereafter
to be associated. His hopes were not in vain. Indeed,
in one respect, he must be held to have even outrivalled
that particular predecessor with whom he has been
oftenest compared. Like *Don Quixote*, *Tom Jones* is the
precursor of a new order of things,—the earliest and
freshest expression of a new departure in art. But

while *Tom Jones* is, to the full, as amusing as *Don Quixote*, it has the advantage of a greatly superior plan, and an interest more skilfully sustained. The incidents which, in Cervantes, simply succeed each other like the scenes in a panorama, are, in *Tom Jones*, but parts of an organised and carefully-arranged progression towards a foreseen conclusion. As the hero and heroine cross and re-cross each other's track, there is scarcely an episode which does not aid in the moving forward of the story. Little details rise lightly and naturally to the surface of the narrative, not more noticeable at first than the most everyday occurrences, and a few pages farther on become of the greatest importance. The hero makes a mock proposal of marriage to Lady Bellaston. It scarcely detains attention, so natural an expedient does it appear, and behold in a chapter or two it has become a terrible weapon in the hands of the injured Sophia! Again, when the secret of Jones' birth[1] is finally disclosed, we look back and discover a hundred little premonitions which escaped us at first, but which, read by the light of our latest knowledge, assume a fresh significance. At the same time, it must be admitted that the over-quoted and somewhat antiquated dictum of Coleridge, by which *Tom Jones* is grouped with the *Alchemist* and *Œdipus Tyrannus*, as one of the three most perfect plots in the world, requires revision. It is impossible to apply the term "perfect"

[1] Much ink has been shed respecting Fielding's reason for making his hero illegitimate. But may not "The History of Tom Jones, a *Foundling*," have had no subtler origin than the recent establishment of the Foundling Hospital, of which Fielding had written in the *Champion*, and in which his friend Hogarth was interested?

to a work which contains such an inexplicable stumbling-
block as the Man of the Hill's story. Then again, progress and animation alone will not make a perfect plot,
unless probability be superadded. And although it cannot be said that Fielding disregards probability, he
certainly strains it considerably. Money is conveniently
lost and found ; the naïvest coincidences continually
occur ; people turn up in the nick of time at the exact
spot required, and develop the most needful (but entirely
casual) relations with the characters. Sometimes an
episode is so inartistically introduced as to be almost
clumsy. Towards the end of the book, for instance,
it has to be shown that Jones has still some power of
resisting temptation, and he accordingly receives from a
Mrs. Arabella Hunt, a written offer of her hand, which
he declines. Mrs. Hunt's name has never been mentioned
before, nor, after this occurrence, is it mentioned again.
But in the brief fortnight which Jones has been in town,
with his head full of Lady Bellaston, Sophia, and the
rest, we are to assume that he has unwittingly inspired
her with so desperate a passion that she proposes and is
refused—all in a chapter. Imperfections of this kind
are more worthy of consideration than some of the
minor negligences which criticism has amused itself by
detecting in this famous book. Such, among others,
is the discovery made by a writer in the *Gentleman's
Magazine*, that in one place winter and summer come too
close together ; or the "strange specimen of oscitancy"
which another (it is, in fact, Mr. Keightley) considers
it worth while to record respecting the misplacing of
the village of Hambrook. To such trifles as these last
the precept of *non offendar maculis* may safely be applied,

although Fielding, wiser than his critics, seems to have
foreseen the necessity for still larger allowances :—

"Cruel indeed," says he in his proemium to Book XI.,
"would it be, if such a Work as this History, which hath employed some Thousands of Hours in the composing, should
be liable to be condemned, because some particular Chapter,
or perhaps Chapters, may be obnoxious to very just and
sensible Objections. . . . To write within such severe Rules
as these, is as impossible as to live up to some splenetic
Opinions ; and if we judge according to the Sentiments of
some Critics, and of some Christians, no Author will be saved
in this World, and no Man in the next."

Notwithstanding its admitted superiority to *Joseph
Andrews* as a work of art, there is no male character in
Tom Jones which can compete with Parson Adams—
none certainly which we regard with equal admiration.
Allworthy, excellent compound of Lyttelton and Allen
though he be, remains always a little stiff and cold in
comparison with the "veined humanity" around him.
We feel of him, as of another impeccable personage, that
we "cannot breathe in that fine air, That pure severity
of perfect light," and that we want the "warmth and
colour" which we find in Adams.   Allworthy is a type
rather than a character—a fault which also seems to
apply to that Molièresque hypocrite, the younger
Blifil.   Fielding seems to have welded this latter
together, rather than to have fused him entire, and
the result is a certain lack of verisimilitude, which
makes us wonder how his pinchbeck professions and
vamped-up virtues could deceive so many persons.
On the other hand, his father, Captain John Blifil,
has all the look of life.   Nor can there be any doubt
about the vitality of Squire Western.   Whether the

germ of his character be derived from Addison's Tory
Foxhunter or not, it is certain that Fielding must have
had superabundant material of his own from which to
model this thoroughly representative, and at the same
time, completely individual character. Western has all
the rustic tastes, the narrow prejudices, the imperfect
education, the unreasoning hatred to the court, which
distinguished the Jacobite country gentleman of the
Georgian era; but his divided love for his daughter
and his horses, his good-humour and his shrewdness,
his foaming impulses and his quick subsidings, his
tears, his oaths, and his barbaric dialect, are all essential
features in a personal portrait. When Jones has rescued
Sophia, he will give him all his stable, the Chevalier
and Miss Slouch excepted; when he finds he is in love
with her, he is in a frenzy to "get *at un*" and "spoil his
Caterwauling." He will have the surgeon's heart's
blood if he takes a drop too much from Sophia's white
arm; when she opposes his wishes as to Blifil, he will
turn her into the street with no more than a smock,
and give his estate to the "*zinking* Fund." Throughout
the book he is *qualis ab incepto*,—boisterous, brutal, jovial,
and inimitable; so that when finally in "Chapter the
Last," we get that pretty picture of him in Sophy's
nursery, protesting that the tattling of his little granddaughter is "sweeter Music than the finest Cry of Dogs
in *England*," we part with him almost with a feeling of
esteem. Scott seems to have thought it unreasonable
that he should have "taken a beating so unresistingly
from the friend of Lord Fellamar," and even hints that
the passage is an interpolation, although he wisely refrains
from suggesting by whom, and should have known that

it was in the first edition. With all deference to so
eminent an authority, it is impossible to share his
hesitation. Fielding was fully aware that even the
bravest have their fits of panic. It must besides be
remembered that Lord Fellamar's friend was not an
effeminate dandy, but a military man—probably a professed *sabreur*, if not a salaried bully like Captain Stab
in the *Rake's Progress;* that he was armed with a stick
and Western was not; and that he fell upon him in
the most unexpected manner, in a place where he was
wholly out of his element. It is inconceivable that the
sturdy squire, with his faculty for distributing "Flicks"
and "Dowses,"—who came so valiantly to the aid of
Jones in his battle-royal with Blifil and Thwackum,—
was likely, under any but very exceptional circumstances, to be dismayed by a cane. It was the exceptional character of the assault which made a coward of
him; and Fielding, who had the keenest eye for inconsistencies of the kind, knew perfectly well what he
was doing.

Of the remaining *dramatis personæ*—the swarming
individualities with which the great comic epic is literally
"all alive," as Lord Monboddo said—it is impossible
to give any adequate account. Few of them, if any, are
open to the objection already pointed out with respect to
Allworthy and the younger Blifil, and most of them bear
signs of having been closely copied from living models.
Parson Thwackum, with his Antinomian doctrines, his
bigotry, and his pedagogic notions of justice; Square
the philosopher, with his faith in human virtue (alas!
poor Square), and his cuckoo-cry about "the unalterable
Rule of Right and the eternal Fitness of Things;" Par-

tridge—the unapproachable Partridge,—with his super-
stition, his vanity, and his perpetual *Infandum regina*,
but who, notwithstanding all his cheap Latinity, cannot construe an unexpected phrase of Horace; Ensign
Northerton, with his vague and disrespectful recollections of "Homo;" young Nightingale and Parson
Supple :—each is a definite character bearing upon his
forehead the mark of his absolute fidelity to human
nature.   Nor are the female actors less accurately
conceived.   Starched Miss Bridget Allworthy, with her
pinched Hogarthian face ; Miss Western, with her dis-
jointed diplomatic jargon ; that budding Slipslop, Mrs.
Honour; worthy Mrs. Miller, Mrs. Fitzpatrick, Mrs.
Waters, Lady Bellaston,—all are to the full as real.
Lady Bellaston especially, deserves more than a word.
Like Lady Booby in *Joseph Andrews*, she is not a pleasant
character; but the picture of the fashionable demirep,
cynical, sensual, and imperious, has never been drawn
more vigorously, or more completely—even by Balzac.
Lastly, there is the adorable Sophia herself, whose pardon
should be asked for naming her in such close proximity
to her frailer sister.   Byron calls her (perhaps with a
slight suspicion of exigence of rhyme) too "emphatic ;"
meaning, apparently, to refer to such passages as her conversation with Mrs. Fitzpatrick, etc.   But the heroine
of Fielding's time—a time which made merry over a
lady's misadventures in horsemanship, and subjected her
to such atrocities as those of Lord Fellamar—required
to be strongly moulded ; and Sophia Western is pure
and womanly, in spite of her unfavourable surroundings.
She is a charming example—the first of her race—of an
unsentimentalised flesh-and-blood heroine ; and Time

has bated no jot of her frank vitality or her healthy
beauty.   Her descendants in the modern novel are far
more numerous than the family which she bore to the
fortunate—the too fortunate—Mr. Jones.

And this reminds us that in the foregoing enumeration we have left out Hamlet.   In truth, it is by no
means easy to speak of this handsome, but very un-
heroic hero.   Lady Mary, employing, curiously enough,
the very phrase which Fielding has made one of his
characters apply to Jones, goes so far as to call him a
"sorry scoundrel;" and eminent critics have dilated upon
his fondness for drink and play.   But it is a notable
instance of the way in which preconceived attributes
are gradually attached to certain characters, that there
is in reality little or nothing to show that he was either
sot or gamester.   With one exception, when, in the joy of
his heart at his benefactor's recovery, he takes too much
wine (and it may be noted that on the same occasion
the Catonic Thwackum drinks considerably more), there
is no evidence that he was specially given to tippling,
even in an age of hard drinkers, while of his gambling
there is absolutely no trace at all.   On the other hand,
he is admittedly brave, generous, chivalrous, kind to
the poor, and courteous to women.   What, then, is his
cardinal defect?   The answer lies in the fact that Fielding, following the doctrine laid down in his initial
chapters, has depicted him under certain conditions (in
which, it is material to note, he is always rather the
tempted than the tempter), with an unvarnished truth-
fulness which to the pure-minded is repugnant, and to the
prurient indecent.   Remembering that he too had been
young, and reproducing, it may be, his own experiences,

he exhibits his youth as he had found him—a " piebald miscellany,"—

  "Bursts of great heart and slips in sensual mire ; "

and, to our modern ideas, when no one dares, as Thackeray complained, " to depict to his utmost power a Man," the spectacle is discomforting. Yet those who look upon human nature as keenly and unflinchingly as Fielding did, knowing how weak and fallible it is,—how prone to fall away by accident or passion,—can scarcely deny the truth of Tom Jones.   That such a person cannot properly serve as a hero now is rather a question of our time than of Fielding's, and it may safely be set aside. One objection which has been made, and made with reason, is that Fielding, while taking care that Nemesis shall follow his hero's lapses, has spoken of them with too much indulgence, or rather without sufficient excuse. Coleridge, who was certainly not squeamish, seems to have felt this when, in a MS. note [1] in the well-known British Museum edition, he says :—

  " Even in this most questionable part of Tom Jones [*i.e.* the Lady Bellaston episode, chap. ix. Book xv.], I cannot but think after frequent reflection on it, that an additional paragraph, more fully & forcibly unfolding Tom Jones's sense of self-degradation on the discovery of the true character of the relation, in which he had stood to Lady Bellaston—& his awakened feeling of the dignity and manliness of Chastity— would have removed in great measure any just objection, at all events relating to Fielding himself, by taking in the state of manners in his time."

---

[1] These notes were communicated by Mr. James Gillman to *The Literary Remains of Samuel Taylor Coleridge*, published by H. N. Coleridge in 1836. The book in which they were made, (it is the four volume edition of 1773, and has Gillman's book-plate), is now in the British Museum. The above transcript is from the MS.

Another point suggested by these last lines may be touched *en passant.* Lady Bellaston, as Fielding has carefully explained (chap. i. Book xiv.), was not a typical, but an exceptional, member of society; and although there were eighteenth-century precedents for such alliances (*e.g.* Miss Edwards and Lord Anne Hamilton, Mrs. Upton and General Braddock,) it is a question whether in a picture of average English life it was necessary to deal with exceptions of this kind, or, at all events, to exemplify them in the principal personage. But the discussion of this subject would prove endless. Right or wrong, Fielding has certainly suffered in popularity for his candour in this respect, since one of the wisest and wittiest books ever written cannot, without hesitation, be now placed in the hands of women or very young people. Moreover, this same candour has undoubtedly attracted to its pages many, neither young nor women, whom its wit finds unintelligent, and its wisdom leaves unconcerned.

But what a brave wit it is, what a wisdom after all, that is contained in this wonderful novel! Where shall we find its like for richness of reflection—for inexhaustible good-humour—for large and liberal humanity! Like Fontenelle, Fielding might fairly claim that he had never cast the smallest ridicule upon the most infinitesimal of virtues; it is against hypocrisy, affectation, insincerity of all kinds, that he wages war. And what a keen and searching observation,—what a perpetual faculty of surprise,—what an endless variety of method! Take the chapter headed ironically *A Receipt to regain the lost Affections of a Wife*, in which Captain John Blifil gives so striking an example of Mr. Samuel Johnson's just pub-

lished *Vanity of Human Wishes*, by dying suddenly of
apoplexy while he is considering what he will do with
Mr. Allworthy's property (when it reverts to him);
or that admirable scene, commended by Macaulay, of
Partridge at the Playhouse, which is none the worse
because it has just a slight look of kinship with that other
famous visit which Sir Roger de Coverley paid to Philips's
Distrest Mother.   Or take again, as utterly unlike either
of these, that burlesque Homeric battle in the church-
yard, where the "sweetly-winding Stour" stands for
"reedy Simois," and the bumpkins round for Greeks
and Trojans!   Or take yet once more, though it is
woful work to offer bricks from this edifice which *has*
already (in a sense) outlived the Escorial,[1] the still more
diverse passage which depicts the changing conflict in
Black George's mind as to whether he shall return to
Jones the sixteen pounds that he has found :—

" *Black George* having received the Purse, set forward towards the Alehouse ; but in the Way a Thought occurred
whether he should not detain this Money likewise.   His
Conscience, however, immediately started at this Suggestion,
and began to upbraid him with Ingratitude to his Benefactor.
To .this his Avarice answered, ' That his conscience should
have considered that Matter before, when he deprived poor
Jones of his 500*l.*   That having quietly acquiesced in what
was of so much greater Importance, it was absurd, if not downright Hypocrisy, to affect any Qualms at this Trifle.'—In
return to which, Conscience, like a good Lawyer, attempted
to distinguish between an absolute Breach of Trust, as here
where the Goods were delivered, and a bare Concealment of
what was found, as in the former Case.   Avarice presently
treated this with Ridicule, called it a Distinction without a
Difference, and absolutely insisted, that when once all Pre-

---

[1] The Escorial, it will be remembered, was partially burned in 1872.

tensions of Honour and Virtue were given up in any one
Instance, that there was no Precedent for resorting to them
upon a second Occasion. In short, poor Conscience had certainly been defeated in the Argument, had not Fear stept in
to her Assistance, and very strenuously urged, that the real
Distinction between the two Actions, did not lie in the different degrees of Honour, but of Safety : For that the secret-
ing the 500l. was a Matter of very little Hazard ; whereas
the detaining the sixteen Guineas was liable to the utmost
Danger of Discovery.

"By this friendly Aid of Fear, Conscience obtained a
compleat Victory in the Mind of *Black George*, and after
making him a few Compliments on his Honesty, forced him
to deliver the Money to *Jones*."

When one remembers that this is but one of many
such passages, and that the book, notwithstanding the
indulgence claimed by the author in the Preface, and
despite a certain hurry at the close, is singularly even
in its workmanship, it certainly increases our respect
for the manly genius of the writer, who, amid all the
distractions of ill-health and poverty, could find the
courage to pursue and perfect such a conception. It
is true that both Cervantes and Bunyan wrote their
immortal works in the confinement of a prison. But
they must at least have enjoyed the seclusion so needful to literary labour ; while *Tom Jones* was written here
and there, at all times and in all places, with the dun
at the door and the wolf not very far from the gate.[1]

The little sentence quoted some pages back from
Walpole's letters is sufficient proof, if proof were needed,
of its immediate success. Andrew Millar was shrewd

[1] Salisbury, in the neighbourhood of which *Tom Jones* is laid,
claims the originals of some of the characters. Thwackum is said
to have been Hele, a schoolmaster; Square, one Chubb, a Deist;
and Dowling the lawyer a person named Stillingfleet.

enough, despite his constitutional confusion, and he is
not likely to have given an additional £100 to the
author of any book without good reason. But the indications of that success are not very plainly impressed
upon the public prints. The *Gentleman's Magazine* for
1749, which, as might be expected from Johnson's connection with it, contains ample accounts of his own
tragedy of *Irene* and Richardson's recently-published
Clarissa, has no notice of *Tom Jones*, nor is there even
any advertisement of the second edition issued in the
same year. But, in the emblematic frontispiece, it
appears under *Clarissa* (and sharing with that work a
possibly unintended proximity to a sprig of laurel stuck
in a bottle of Nantes), among a pile of the books of
the year; and in the "poetical essays" for August,
one Thomas Cawthorn breaks into rhymed panegyric.
"Sick of her fools," sings this enthusiastic but scarcely
lucid admirer—

> "Sick of her fools, great *Nature* broke the jest,
> And *Truth* held out each character to test,
> When *Genius* spoke : Let *Fielding* take the pen !
> Life dropt her mask, and all mankind were men."

There were others, however, who would scarcely
have echoed the laudatory sentiments of Mr. Cawthorn.
Among these was again the excellent Richardson, who
seems to have been wholly unpropitiated by the olive
branch held out to him in the *Jacobite's Journal*. His
vexation at the indignity put upon *Pamela* by *Joseph
Andrews* was now complicated by a twittering jealousy of
the "spurious brat," as he obligingly called *Tom Jones*,
whose success had been so "unaccountable." In these
circumstances, some of the letters of his correspondents

must have been gall and wormwood to him. Lady Bradshaigh, for instance, under her *nom de plume* of "Belfour," tells him that she is fatigued with the very name of the book, having met several young ladies who were for ever talking of their Tom Jones's, "for so they call their favourites," and that the gentlemen, on their side, had their Sophias, one having gone so far as to give that all-popular name to his "Dutch mastiff puppy." But perhaps the best and freshest exhibition (for, as far as can be ascertained, it has never hitherto been made public) of Richardson's attitude to his rival is to be found in a little group of letters in the Forster collection at South Kensington. The writers are Aaron Hill and his daughters; but the letters do not seem to have been known to Mrs. Barbauld, whose last communication from Hill is dated November 2, 1748. Nor are they to be found in Hill's own Correspondence. The ladies, it appears, had visited Richardson at Salisbury Court in 1741, and were great admirers of *Pamela*, and the "divine *Clarissa*." Some months after *Tom Jones* was published, Richardson (not yet having brought himself to read the book) had asked them to do so, and give him their opinion as to its merits. Thereupon Minerva and Astræa, who despite their names, and their description of themselves as "Girls of an untittering Disposition," must have been very bright and lively young persons, began seriously "to lay their two wise heads together" and "hazard this Discovery of their Emptiness." Having "with much ado got over some Reluctance, that was bred by a familiar coarseness in the *Title*," they report "much (masqu'd) merit" in the "whole six volumes"—"a double merit, both of Head, and *Heart*."

Had it been the latter only it would be more worthy
of Mr. Richardson's perusal; but, say these considerate
pioneers, if he does spare it his attention, he must
only do so at his leisure, for the author "introduces
All his Sections (and too often interweaves the *serious*
Body of his meanings), with long Runs of bantering
Levity, which his [Fielding's] Good sense may suffer
by Effect of." "It is true (they continue), he seems to
wear this Lightness, as a grave Head sometime wears a
Feather: which tho' He and Fashion may consider as
an ornament, Reflection will condemn, as a Disguise,
and *covering*." Then follows a brief excursus, intended
for their correspondent's special consolation, upon the
folly of treating grave things lightly; and with delightful sententiousness the letter thus concludes :—

"Mean while, it is an honest pleasure, which we take in
adding, that (exclusive of one wild, detach'd, and independent Story of a *Man of the Hill*, that neither brings on Anything, nor rose from Anything that went before it) All the
changefull windings of the Author's Fancy carry on a course
of regular Design; and end in an extremely moving Close,
where Lives that seem'd to wander and run different ways,
meet, All, in an instructive Center.

"The whole Piece consists of an inventive Race of Dis-
apointments and Recoveries. It excites Curiosity, and
holds it watchful. It has just and pointed Satire; but it is
a partial Satire, and confin'd, too narrowly : It sacrifices to
Authority, and Interest. Its *Events* reward Sincerity, and
punish and expose Hypocrisy; shew Pity and Benevolence in
amiable Lights, and Avarice and Brutality in very despicable
ones. In every Part It has Humanity for its Intention: In
too many, it *seems* wantoner than It was meant to be: It has
bold shocking Pictures; and (I fear) [1] not unresembling ones,
in high Life, and in low. And (to conclude this too adven-

---

[1] The "pen-holder" is the fair Astræa.

turous Guess-work, from a Pair of forward Baggages) woud,
every where, (we think,) *deserve* to please,—if stript of what
the Author thought himself most sure to *please by.*

" And thus, Sir, we have told you our sincere opinion of
Tom Jones. . . .

" Your most profest Admirers and most humble Servants,

" Astræa ⎫
    and   ⎬ Hill.
Minerva ⎭

" PLAISTOW *the* 27*th of July* 1749."

Richardson's reply to this ingenuous criticism is
dated the 4th of August. His requesting two young
women to study and criticise a book which he has
heard strongly condemned as immoral,—his own obvious
familiarity with what he has not read but does not
scruple to censure,—his transparently jealous anticipation of its author's ability,—all this forms a picture so
characteristic alike of the man and the time that no
apology is needed for the following textual extract :—

"I must confess, that I have been prejudiced by the Opinion
of Several judicious Friends against the truly coarse-titled
Tom Jones ; and so have been discouraged from reading it.—I
was told, that it was a rambling Collection of Waking Dreams,
in which Probability was not observed : And that it had a very
bad Tendency. And I had Reason to think that the Author
intended for his Second View (His *first*, to fill his Pocket, by
accommodating it to the reigning Taste) in writing it, to
whiten a vicious Character, and to make Morality bend to his
Practices. What Reason had he to make his Tom illegitimate,
in an Age where Keeping is become a Fashion ? Why did
he make him a common—What shall I call it ? And a Kept
Fellow, the Lowest of all Fellows, yet in Love with a Young
Creature who was traping [trapesing ?] after him, a Fugitive
from her Father's House ?—Why did he draw his Heroine so
fond, so foolish, and so insipid ?—Indeed he has one Excuse
—He knows not how to draw a delicate Woman—He has
not been accustomed to such Company,—And is too prescrib-

ing, too impetuous, too immoral, I will venture to say, to take
any other Byass than that a perverse and crooked Nature has
given him ; or Evil Habits, at least, have confirm'd in him.
Do Men expect Grapes of Thorns, or Figs of Thistles ? But,
perhaps, I think the worse of the Piece because I know the
Writer, and dislike his Principles both Public and Private,
tho' I wish well to the *Man*, and Love Four worthy Sisters
of his,[1] with whom I am well acquainted. And indeed should
admire him, did he make the Use of his Talents which I
wish him to make, For the Vein of Humour, and Ridicule,
which he is Master of, might, if properly turned do great
Service to ye Cause of Virtue.

"But no more of this Gentleman's Work, after I have said,
That the favourable Things, you say of the Piece, will tempt
me, if I can find Leisure, to give it a Perusal."

Notwithstanding this last sentence, Richardson more
than once reverts to *Tom Jones* before he finishes his
letter. Its effect upon Minerva and Astræa is best
described in an extract from Aaron Hill's reply, dated
seven days later (August the 11th) :—

" Unfortunate *Tom Jones!* how sadly has he mortify'd Two
sawcy Correspondents of your making ! They are with me
now : and bid me tell you, You have spoil'd 'em Both, for
Criticks.—Shall I add, a Secret which they did not bid me
tell you ?—They, Both, fairly *cry'd*, that You shou'd think it
possible they cou'd approve of Any thing, in Any work, that
had an *Evil Tendency*, in any Part or Purpose of it. They
maintain their Point so far, however, as to be convinc'd they
say, that *you* will disapprove this over-rigid Judgment of
those Friends, who cou'd not find a Thread of Moral Meaning
in Tom Jones, quite independent of the Levities they justly
censure.—And, as soon as you have Time to read him,
for yourself, tis there, pert Sluts, they will be bold enough
to rest the Matter.—Mean while, they love and honour you
and your opinions."

---

[1] From this it would seem that General Fielding had some
daughters of whom no record has been preserved.

To this the author of *Clarissa* replied by writing a
long epistle deploring the pain he had given the "dear
Ladies," and minutely justifying his foregone conclusions
from the expressions they had used. He refers to Fielding again as " a very indelicate, a very impetuous, an
unyielding-spirited Man ;" and he also trusts to be able
to " bestow a Reading" on *Tom Jones ;* but by a letter
from Lady Bradshaigh, printed in Barbauld, and dated
December 1749, it seems that even at that date he had
not, or pretended he had not, yet done so. In another
of the unpublished South Kensington letters, from a Mr.
Solomon Lowe, occurs the following :—" I do not doubt "
—says the writer—"but all Europe will ring of it [*Clarissa*]: when a Cracker, that was some thous^{d} hours a-com-
posing,[1] will no longer be heard, or talkt-of." Richardson,
with business-like precision, has gravely docketed this
in his own handwriting,—"Cracker, T. Jones."

It is unfortunate for Mr. Lowe's reputation as a
prophet that, after more than one hundred and thirty
years, this ephemeral firework, as he deemed it, should
still be sparkling with undiminished brilliancy, and to
judge by recent editions, is selling as vigorously as ever.
From the days when Lady Mary wrote " *Ne plus ultra* "
in her own copy, and La Harpe called it *le premier roman
du monde*, (a phrase which, by the way, De Musset applies
to *Clarissa*), it has come down to us with an almost
universal accompaniment of praise. Gibbon, Byron,
Coleridge, Scott, Dickens, Thackeray,—have all left their
admiration on record,—to say nothing of professional
critics innumerable. As may be seen from the British
Museum Catalogue, it has been translated into French,

[1] *Vide Tom Jones*, Book xi. chap. i.

German, Polish, Dutch, and Spanish. Russia and Sweden
have also their versions. The first French translation,
or rather abridgment, by M. de La Place was prohibited in France (to Richardson's delight) by royal
decree, an act which affords another instance, in Scott's
words, of that "French delicacy, which, on so many
occasions, has strained at a gnat, and swallowed a
camel" (*e.g.* the novels of M. Crébillon *fils*). La
Place's edition (1750) was gracefully illustrated with
sixteen plates by Hubert Bourguignon, called Gravelot,
one of those eighteenth - century illustrators whose
designs at present are the rage in Paris. In England,
Fielding's best-known pictorial interpreters are Row-
landson and Cruikshank, the latter being by far the
more sympathetic. Stothard also prepared some designs
for Harrison's *Novelist's Magazine ;* but his refined and
effeminate pencil was scarcely strong enough for the task.
Hogarth alone could have been the ideal illustrator of
Henry Fielding; that is to say—if, in lieu of the rude
designs he made for *Tristram Shandy*, he could have been
induced to undertake the work in the larger fashion
of the *Rake's Progress*, or *The Marriage à la Mode*.

As might perhaps be anticipated, *Tom Jones* attracted
the dramatist.[1] In 1765, one J. H. Steffens made a
comedy of it for the German boards ; and in 1785,
a M. Desforges based upon it another, called *Tom*

---

[1] It may be added that it also attracted the plagiarist. As
Pamela had its sequel in *Pamela's Conduct in High Life*, 1741, so
Tom Jones was continued in *The History of Tom Jones the Foundling,
in his Married State*, a second edition of which was issued in 1750.
The Preface announces, needlessly enough, that "Henry Fielding,
Esq., is not the Author of this Book." It deserves no serious con-
sideration.

Jones à Londres, which was acted at the *Théâtre Fran çais.* It was also turned into a comic opera by Joseph Reed in 1769, and played at Covent Garden. But its most piquant transformation is the *Comédie lyrique* of Poinsinet, acted at Paris in 1765-6 to the lively music of Philidor. The famous Caillot took the part of Squire Western, who, surrounded by *piqueurs,* and girt with the conventional *cor de chasse* of the Gallic sportsman, sings the following *ariette,* diversified with true Fontainebleau terms of venery :—

> " D'un Cerf, dix Cors, j'ai connaissance :
> On l'attaque au fort, on le lance ;
> Tous sont prêts :
> Piqueurs & Valets
> Suivent les pas de l'ami Jone *(sic).*
> J'entends crier : Volcelets, Volcelets.
> Aussitôt j'ordonne
> Que la Meute donne.
> Tayaut, Tayaut, Tayaut.
> Mes chiens découplés l'environnent ;
> Les trompes sonnent :
> ' Courage, Amis : Tayaut, Tayaut.'
> Quelques chiens, que l'ardeur dérange,
> Quittent la voye & prennent le change.
> Jones les rassure d'un cri :
> Ourvari, ourvari.
> Accoute, accoute, accoute.
> Au retour nous en revoyons.
> Accoute, à Mirmiraut, courons ;
> Tout à Griffaut ;
> Y après : Tayaut, Tayaut.
> On reprend route,
> Voilà le Cerf à l'eau.
> La trompe sonne,
> La Meute donne,
> L'écho résonne,

Nous pressons les nouveaux relais :
Volcelets, Volcelets.
L'animal forcé succombe,
Fait un effort, se releve, enfin tombe :
Et nos chasseurs chantent tous à l'envi :
' Amis, goûtons les fruits de la victoire ;
' Amis, Amis, célébrons notre gloire.
' Halali, Fanfare, Halali
' Halali.' "

With this triumphant flourish of trumpets the present chapter may be fittingly concluded.

CHAPTER VI.

JUSTICE LIFE—AMELIA.

In one of Horace Walpole's letters to George Montagu, already quoted, there is a description of Fielding's Bow Street establishment, which has attracted more attention than it deserves. The letter is dated May the 18th, 1749, and the passage (in Cunningham's edition) runs as follows :—

"He [Rigby] and Peter Bathurst [1] t'other night carried a servant of the latter's, who had attempted to shoot him, before Fielding ; who, to all his other vocations, has, by the grace of Mr. Lyttelton, added that of Middlesex justice. He sent them word he was at supper, that they must come next morning. They did not understand that freedom, and ran up, where they found him banqueting with a blind man, a whore, and three Irishmen, on some cold mutton and a bone of ham, both in one dish, and the dirtiest cloth. He never stirred nor asked them to sit. Rigby, who had seen him so often come to beg a guinea of Sir C. Williams, and Bathurst, at whose father's he had lived for victuals, understood that dig-

---

[1] Bathurst was M.P. for New Sarum, and brother of Pope's friend, Allen, Lord Bathurst. Rigby was the Richard Rigby whose despicable character is familiar in Eighteenth-Century Memoirs. "He died (says Cunningham) involved in debt, with his accounts as Paymaster of the Forces hopelessly unsettled."

nity as little, and pulled themselves chairs; on which he civilised."

Scott calls this "a humiliating anecdote;" and both Mr. Lawrence and Mr. Keightley have exhausted rhetoric in the effort to explain it away. As told, it is certainly uncomplimentary; but considerable deductions must be made, both for the attitude of the narrator and the occasion of the narrative. Walpole's championship of his friends was notorious; and his absolute injustice, when his partisan spirit was uppermost, is everywhere patent to the readers of his Letters. In the present case he was not of the encroaching party; and he speaks from hearsay solely. But his friends had, in his opinion, been outraged by a man, who, according to his ideas of fitness, should have come to them cap in hand; and as a natural consequence, the story, no doubt exaggerated when it reached him, loses nothing under his transforming and malicious pen. Stripped of its decorative flippancy, however, there remains but little that can really be regarded as "humiliating." Scott himself suggests, what is most unquestionably the case, that the blind man was the novelist's half-brother, afterwards Sir John Fielding; and it is extremely unlikely that the lady so discourteously characterised could have been any other than his wife, who, Lady Stuart tells us, "had few personal charms." There remain the "three Irishmen," who may, or may not, have been perfectly presentable members of society. At all events, their mere nationality, so rapidly decided upon, cannot be regarded as a stigma. That the company and entertainment were scarcely calculated to suit the superfine standard of Mr. Bathurst and Mr. Rigby may perhaps be conceded. Fielding was by no means a

rich man, and in his chequered career had possibly grown
indifferent to minor decencies. Moreover, we are told
by Murphy that, as a Westminster justice, he "kept his
table open to those who had been his friends when young,
and had impaired their own fortunes." Thus, it must
always have been a more or less ragged regiment who
met about that kindly Bow Street board; but that the
fact reflects upon either the host or guests cannot be
admitted for a moment. If the anecdote is discreditable
to anyone it is to that facile retailer of *ana* and incorrigible
society-gossip, Mr. Horace Walpole.

But while these unflattering tales were told of his
private life, Fielding was fast becoming eminent in his
public capacity. On the 12th of May 1749 he was
unanimously chosen chairman of Quarter Sessions at
Hicks's Hall (as the Clerkenwell Sessions House was then
called); and on the 29th of June following he delivered
a charge to the Westminster Grand Jury which is usually
printed with his works, and which is still regarded by
lawyers as a model exposition. It is at first a little
unexpected to read his impressive and earnest denuncia-
tions of masquerades and theatres (in which latter, by
the way, one Samuel Foote had very recently been following the example of the author of *Pasquin*); but Fielding the magistrate and Fielding the playwright were
two different persons; and a long interval of changeful
experience lay between them. In another part of his
charge, which deals with the offence of libelling, it is
possible that his very vigorous appeal was not the less
forcible by reason of the personal attacks to which he
had referred in the Preface to *David Simple*, the *Jacobite's
Journal*, and elsewhere. His only other literary efforts

during this year appear to have been a little pamphlet
entitled *A True State of the Case of Bosavern Penlez ;* and
a formal congratulatory letter to Lyttelton upon his
second marriage, in which, while speaking gratefully of
his own obligations to his friend, he endeavours to enlist
his sympathies for Moore the fabulist who was also
"about to marry." The pamphlet had reference to an
occurrence which took place in July. Three sailors of the
"Grafton" man-of-war had been robbed in a house of ill
fame in the Strand. Failing to obtain redress, they
attacked the house with their comrades, and wrecked it,
causing a "dangerous riot," to which Fielding makes
incidental reference in one of his letters to the Duke of
Bedford, and which was witnessed by John Byrom, the
poet and stenographer, in whose *Remains* it is described.
Bosavern Penlez or Pen Lez, who had joined the crowd,
and in whose possession some of the stolen property was
found, was tried and hanged in September. His sentence,
which was considered extremely severe, excited much
controversy, and the object of Fielding's pamphlet was
to vindicate the justice and necessity of his conviction.

Towards the close of 1749 Fielding fell seriously ill
with fever aggravated by gout. It was indeed at one
time reported that mortification had supervened ; but
under the care of Dr. Thomson, that dubious practitioner
whose treatment of Winnington in 1746 had given rise
to so much paper war, he recovered ; and during 1750
was actively employed in his magisterial duties. At
this period lawlessness and violence appear to have
prevailed to an unusual extent in the metropolis, and
the office of a Bow Street justice was no sinecure.
Reform of some kind was felt on all sides to be urgently

required ; and Fielding threw his two years' experience
and his deductions therefrom into the form of a pamphlet
entitled *An Enquiry into the Causes of the late Increase of
Robbers, etc., with some Proposals for remedying this growing
Evil.* It was dedicated to the then Lord High Chancellor,
Philip Yorke, Lord Hardwicke, by whom, as well as by
more recent legal authórities, it was highly appreciated.
Like the *Charge to the Grand Jury*, it is a grave argumen-
tative document, dealing seriously with luxury, drunk-
enness, gaming, and other prevalent vices.   Once only,
in an ironical passage respecting beaus and fine ladies,
does the author remind us of the author of *Tom Jones.*
As a rule, he is weighty, practical, and learned in the
law.   Against the curse of Gin - drinking, which, owing
to the facilities for obtaining that liquor, had increased
to an alarming extent among the poorer classes, he is
especially urgent and energetic.   He points out that it
is not only making dreadful havoc in the present, but
that it is enfeebling the race of the future, and he concludes—

"Some little Care on this Head is surely necessary : For
tho' the Encrease of Thieves, and the Destruction of Morality ; though the Loss of our Labourers, our Sailors, and our
Soldiers, should not be sufficient Reasons, there is one which
seems to be unanswerable, and that is, the Loss of our Gin-
drinkers : Since, should the drinking this Poison be continued
in its present Height during the next twenty Years, there
will, by that Time, be very few of the common People left to
drink it."

To the appeal thus made by Fielding in January 1751,
Hogarth added his pictorial protest in the following
month by his awful plate of *Gin Lane*, which, if not
actually prompted by his friend's words, was certainly

inspired by the same crying evil. One good result of
these efforts was the "Bill for restricting the Sale of
Spirituous Liquors," to which the royal assent was given
in June, and Fielding's connection with this enactment
is practically acknowledged by Horace Walpole in his
Memoires of the Last ten Years of the Reign of George II. The
law was not wholly effectual, and was difficult to enforce;
but it was not by any means without its good effects.[1]

Between the publication of the *Enquiry* and that of
Amelia there is nothing of importance to chronicle except
Fielding's connection with one of the events of 1751, the
discovery of the Glastonbury waters. According to the
account given in the *Gentleman's* for July in that year, a
certain Matthew Chancellor had been cured of "an asthma
and phthisic" of thirty years' standing by drinking from
a spring near Chain Gate, Glastonbury, to which he had
(so he alleged) been directed in a dream. The spring
forthwith became famous; and in May an entry in the
Historical Chronicle for Sunday, the 5th, records that
above 10,000 persons had visited it, deserting Bristol,
Bath, and other popular resorts. Numerous pamphlets

[1] The Rev. R. Hurd, afterwards Bishop of Worcester, an upright
and scholarly, but formal and censorious man, whom Johnson
called a "word-picker," and franker contemporaries "an old maid
in breeches," has left a reference to Fielding at this time which is
not flattering. "I dined with him [Ralph Allen] yesterday,
where I met Mr. Fielding,—a poor emaciated, worn-out rake, whose
gout and infirmities have got the better even of his buffoonery"
(Letter to Balguy, dated "Inner Temple, 19th March, 1751.")
That Fielding had not long before been dangerously ill, and that
he was a martyr to gout, is fact: the rest is probably no more than
the echo of a foregone conclusion, based upon report, or dislike to
his works. Hurd praised Richardson and proscribed Sterne. He
must have been wholly out of sympathy with the author of *Tom
Jones.*

were published for and against the new waters; and
a letter in their favour, which appeared in the *London
Daily Advertiser* for the 31st August, signed "Z. Z.," is
"supposed to be wrote" by "J——e F——g." Fielding
was, as may be remembered, a Somersetshire man, Sharpham Park, his birthplace, being about three miles from
Glastonbury; and he testifies to the "wonderful Effects of
this salubrious Spring" in words which show that he had
himself experienced them. "Having seen great Numbers
of my Fellow Creatures under two of the most miserable
Diseases human Nature can labour under, the Asthma and
Evil, return from *Glastonbury* blessed with the Return of
Health, and having myself been relieved from a Disorder
which baffled the most skilful Physicians," justice to
mankind (he says) obliges him to take notice of the subject. The letter is interesting, more as showing that, at
this time, Fielding's health was broken, than as proving
the efficacy of the cure; for, whatever temporary relief
the waters afforded, it is clear (as Mr. Lawrence pertinently remarks) that he derived no permanent benefit
from them. They must, however, have continued to
attract visitors, as a pump-room was opened in August
1753; and, although they have now fallen into disuse,
they were popular for many years.

But a more important occurrence than the discovery
of the Somersetshire spring is a little announcement
contained in Sylvanus Urban's list of publications for
December 1751, No. 17 of which is "*Amelia*, in 4 books,
12mo; by Henry Fielding, Esq." The publisher, of
course, was Andrew Millar; and the actual day of issue,
as appears from the *General Advertiser*, was December the
19th, although the title-page, by anticipation, bore the

date of 1752.   There were two mottoes, one of which was
the appropriate—

> " *Felices ter & amplius*
> *Quos irrupta tenet Copula ;*"

and the dedication, brief and simply expressed, was to
Ralph Allen.   As before, the "artful aid" of advertisement was invoked to whet the public appetite.

" To satisfy the earnest Demand of the Publick (says
Millar), this Work has been printed at four Presses ; but the
Proprietor notwithstanding finds it impossible to get them (*sic*)
bound in Time, without spoiling the Beauty of the Impression,
and therefore will sell them sew'd at Half-a-Guinea."

This was open enough ; but, according to Scott, Millar
adopted a second expedient to assist *Amelia* with the
booksellers.

" He had paid a thousand pounds for the copyright ; and
when he began to suspect that the work would be judged
inferior to its predecessor, he employed the following stratagem
to push it upon the trade.   At a sale made to the booksellers,
previous to the publication, Millar offered his friends his other
publications on the usual terms of discount ; but when he
came to *Amelia*, he laid it aside, as a work expected to be in
such demand, that he could not afford to deliver it to the trade
in the usual manner.   The *ruse* succeeded—the impression
was anxiously bought up, and the bookseller relieved from
every apprehension of a slow sale."

There were several reasons why—superficially speaking
—*Amelia* should be " judged inferior to its predecessor."
That it succeeded *Tom Jones* after an interval of little
more than two years and eight months would be an
important element in the comparison, if it were known
at all definitely what period was occupied in writing *Tom
Jones*.   All that can be affirmed is that Fielding must have

been far more at leisure when he composed the earlier
work than he could possibly have been when filling the
office of a Bow Street magistrate. But, in reality, there is
a much better explanation of the superiority of *Tom Jones*
to *Amelia* than the merely empirical one of the time it took.
Tom Jones, it has been admirably said by a French critic,
" *est la condensation et le résumé de toute une existence. C'est
le résultat et la conclusion de plusieurs années de passions et
de pensées, la formule dernière et compléte de la philosophie
personnelle que l'on s'est faite sur tout ce que l'on a vu et
senti.*" Such an experiment, argues Planche, is not twice
repeated in a lifetime : the soil which produced so rich
a crop can but yield a poorer aftermath. Behind *Tom
Jones* there was the author's ebullient youth and man-
hood ; behind *Amelia* but a section of his graver middle-
age. There are other reasons for diversity in the manner of the book itself. The absence of the initial chapters, which gave so much variety to *Tom Jones*, tends to
heighten the sense of impatience which, it must be con-
fessed, occasionally creeps over the reader of *Amelia*,
especially in those parts where, like Dickens at a later
period, Fielding delays the progress of his narrative for
the discussion of social problems and popular grievances.
However laudable the desire (expressed in the dedication)
" to expose some of the most glaring Evils, as well public
as private, which at present infest this Country," the result
in *Amelia*, from an art point of view, is as unsatisfactory
as that of certain well-known pages of *Bleak House* and
Little Dorrit. Again, there is a marked change in the
attitude of the author,—a change not wholly reconcilable
with the brief period which separates the two novels.
However it may have chanced, whether from failing health

or otherwise, the Fielding of *Amelia* is suddenly a far older man than the Fielding of *Tom Jones*. The robust and irrepressible vitality, the full-veined delight of living, the energy of observation and strength of satire, which characterise the one give place in the other to a calmer retrospection, a more compassionate humanity, a gentler and more benignant criticism of life. That, as some have contended, *Amelia* shows an intellectual falling-off cannot for a moment be admitted, least of all upon the ground—as even so staunch an admirer as Mr. Keightley has allowed himself to believe—that certain of its incidents are obviously repeated from the *Modern Husband* and others of the author's plays. At this rate *Tom Jones* might be judged inferior to *Joseph Andrews*, because the Political Apothecary in the "Man of the Hill's" story has his prototype in the *Coffee-House Politician*, whose original is Addison's Upholsterer. The plain fact is, that Fielding recognised the failure of his plays as literature; he regarded them as dead; and freely transplanted what was good of his forgotten work into the work which he hoped would live. In this, it may be, there was something of indolence or haste; but assuredly there was no proof of declining powers.

If, for the sake of comparison, *Tom Jones* may be described as an animated and happily-constructed comedy, with more than the usual allowance of first-rate characters, *Amelia* must be regarded as a one-part piece, in which the rest of the *dramatis personæ* are wholly subordinate to the central figure. Captain Booth, the two Colonels, Atkinson and his wife, Miss Matthews, Dr. Harrison, Trent, the shadowy and maleficent "My Lord," are all less active on their own account than energised and set in motion by Amelia. Round her they revolve ; from her they obtain their impulse and their orbit. The best of the men, as studies, are Dr. Harrison and Colonel Bath. The former, who is as benevolent as Allworthy, is far more human, and it may be added, more humorous in well-doing. He is an individual rather than an abstraction. Bath, with his dignity and gun-cotton honour, is also admirable, but not entirely free from the objection made to some of Dickens's creations, that they are rather characteristics than characters. Captain William Booth, beyond his truth to nature, manifests no qualities that can compensate for his weakness, and the best that can be said of him is, that without it, his wife would have had no opportunity for the display of her magnanimity. There is also a certain want of consistency in his presentment ; and when, in the residence of Mr. Bondum the bailiff, he suddenly develops an unexpected scholarship, it is impossible not to suspect that Fielding was unwilling to lose the opportunity of preserving some neglected scenes of the *Author's Farce*. Miss Matthews is a new and remarkable study of the *femme entretenue*, to parallel which, as in the case of Lady Bellaston, we must go to Balzac ; Mrs. James, again, is an excellent example of that vapid and colourless nonentity, the " person of condition." Mrs. Bennet, although apparently more contradictory and less intelligible, is nevertheless true to her past history and present environments ; while her husband, the sergeant, with his concealed and reverential love for his beautiful foster-sister, has had a long line of descendants in the modern novel. It is upon Amelia, however, that the author has lavished all his pains, and there is no more touching

portrait in the whole of fiction than this heroic and
immortal one of feminine goodness and forbearance. It is
needless to repeat that it is painted from Fielding's first
wife, or to insist that, as Lady Mary was fully persuaded,
" several of the incidents he mentions are real matters of
fact." That famous scene where Amelia is spreading,
for the recreant who is losing his money at the King's
Arms, the historic little supper of hashed mutton which
she has cooked with her own hands, and denying herself
a glass of white wine to save the paltry sum of sixpence,
" while her Husband was paying a Debt of several
Guineas incurred by the Ace of Trumps being in the
Hands of his Adversary "—a scene which it is impossible
to read aloud without a certain huskiness in the throat,
—the visits to the pawnbroker and the sponging-house,
the robbery by the little servant, the encounter at
Vauxhall, and some of the pretty vignettes of the children, are no doubt founded on personal recollections.
Whether the pursuit to which the heroine is exposed
had any foundation in reality it is impossible to say ;
and there is a passage in Murphy's memoir which almost
reads as if it had been penned with the express purpose
of anticipating any too harshly literal identification of
Booth with Fielding, since we are told of the latter that
"though disposed to gallantry by his strong animal
spirits, and the vivacity of his passions, he was remarkable for tenderness *and constancy to his wife* [the italics
are ours], and the strongest affection for his children."
These, however, are questions beside the matter, which
is the conception of *Amelia.* That remains, and must
remain for ever, in the words of one of Fielding's greatest
modern successors, a figure

> " wrought with love . . .
> Nought modish in it, pure and noble lines
> Of generous womanhood that fits all time."

There are many women who forgive ; but Amelia does
more—she not only forgives, but she forgets. The
passage in which she exhibits to her contrite husband
the letter received long before from Miss Matthews is
one of the noblest in literature ; and if it had been
recorded that Fielding—like Thackeray on a memorable
occasion—had here slapped his fist upon the table, and
said " *That* is a stroke of genius !" it would scarcely
have been a thing to be marvelled at. One final point
in connection with her may be noted, which has not
always been borne in mind by those who depict good
women — much after Hogarth's fashion — without a
head. She is not by any means a simpleton, and
it is misleading to describe her as a tender, fluttering
little creature, who, because she can cook her husband's
supper, and caresses him with the obsolete name of
Billy, must necessarily be contemptible. On the contrary, she has plenty of ability and good sense, with a
fund of humour which enables her to slily enjoy and
even gently satirise the fine lady airs of Mrs. James.
Nor is it necessary to contend that her faculties are
subordinated to her affections ; but rather that conjugal
fidelity and Christian charity are inseparable alike from
her character and her creed.

As illustrating the tradition that Fielding depicted
his first wife in Sophia Western and in Amelia, it has
been remarked that there is no formal description of her
personal appearance in his last novel, her portrait having
already been drawn at length in *Tom Jones*. But the

following depreciatory sketch by Mrs. James is worth
quoting, not only because it indirectly conveys the impression of a very handsome woman, but because it
is also an admirable specimen of Fielding's lighter
manner :—

" ' In the first place,' cries Mrs. James, ' her eyes are too
large ; and she hath a look with them that I don't know how
to describe ; but I know I don't like it.   Then her eyebrows
are too large ; therefore, indeed, she doth all in her power to
remedy this with her pincers ; for if it was not for those, her
eyebrows would be preposterous.—Then her nose, as well
proportioned as it is, has a visible scar on one side.[1]—Her
neck likewise is too protuberant for the genteel size, especially
as she laces herself ; for no woman, in my opinion, can be
genteel who is not entirely flat before.   And lastly, she is
both too short, and too tall.—Well, you may laugh, Mr.
James, I know what I mean, though I cannot well express it.
I mean, that she is too tall for a pretty woman, and too short
for a fine woman.—There is such a thing as a kind of insipid
medium—a kind of something that is neither one thing or
another.   I know not how to express it more clearly ; but
when I say such a one is a pretty woman, a pretty thing, a
pretty creature, you know very well I mean a little woman ;
and when I say such a one is a very fine woman, a very fine
person of a woman, to be sure I must mean a tall woman.
Now a woman that is between both, is certainly neither the
one nor the other."

The ingenious expedients of Andrew Millar, to which
reference has been made, appear to have so far succeeded that a new edition of *Amelia* was called for on
the day of publication. Johnson, to whom we owe
this story, was thoroughly captivated with the book.
Notwithstanding that on another occasion he paradoxi-
cally asserted that the author was " a blockhead "—

---

[1] See note on this subject in chapter iv.

"a barren rascal," he read it through without stopping,
and pronounced Mrs. Booth to be "the most pleasing
heroine of all the romances." Richardson, on the other
hand, found "the characters and situations so wretch-
edly low and dirty" that he could not get farther than
the first volume. With the professional reviewers, a
certain Criticulus in the *Gentleman's* excepted, it seems to
have fared but ill; and although these adverse verdicts,
if they exist, are now more or less inaccessible, Fielding
has apparently summarised most of them in a mock-trial
of *Amelia* before the "*Court of* Censorial Enquiry," the
proceedings of which are recorded in Nos. 7 and 8 of the
Covent-Garden Journal. The book is indicted upon the
Statute of Dulness, and the heroine is charged with
being a "*low* Character," a "Milksop" and a "*Fool;*"
with lack of spirit and fainting too frequently; with
dressing her children, cooking and other "servile Offices;"
with being too forgiving to her husband; and lastly,
as may be expected, with the inconsistency, already
amply referred to, of being "a Beauty *without a nose.*"
Dr. Harrison and Colonel Bath are arraigned much in
the same fashion. After some evidence against her has
been tendered, and "a Great Number of Beaus, Rakes,
fine Ladies, and several formal Persons with bushy Wigs,
and Canes at their Noses," are preparing to supplement
it, a grave man steps forward, and, begging to be heard,
delivers what must be regarded as Fielding's final apology
for his last novel :—

"If you, Mr. Censor, are yourself a Parent, you will view
me with Compassion when I declare I am the Father of this
poor Girl the Prisoner at the Bar; nay, when I go further
and avow, that of all my Offspring she is my favourite Child.

I can truly say that I bestowed a more than ordinary Pains in her Education ; in which I will venture to affirm, I followed the Rules of all those who are acknowledged to have writ best on the Subject ; and if her Conduct be fairly examined, she will be found to deviate very little from the strictest Observation of all those Rules ; neither Homer nor Virgil pursued them with greater Care than myself, and the candid and learned Reader will see that the latter was the noble model, which I made use of on this Occasion.

"I do not think my Child is entirely free from Faults. I know nothing human that is so ; but surely she doth not deserve the Rancour with which she hath been treated by the Public. However, it is not my Intention, at present, to make any Defence ; but shall submit to a Compromise, which hath been always allowed in this Court in all Prosecutions for Dulness. I do, therefore, solemnly declare to you, Mr. Censor, that I will trouble the World no more with any Children of mine by the same Muse."

Whether sincere or not, this last statement appears to have afforded the greatest gratification to Richardson. "Will I leave you to Captain Booth?" he writes triumphantly to Mrs. Donnellan, in answer to a question she had put to him. "Captain Booth, Madam, has done his own business. Mr. Fielding has over-written himself, or rather *under*-written ; and in his own journal seems ashamed of his last piece ; and has promised that the same Muse shall write no more for him. The piece, in short, is as dead as if it had been published forty years ago, as to sale." There is much to the same effect in the worthy little printer's correspondence ; but enough has been quoted to show how intolerable to the super-sentimental creator of the high-souled and heroic Clarissa was his rival's plainer and more practical picture of matronly virtue and modesty. In cases of this kind, *parva seges satis est*, and Amelia has long since outlived both rival malice and contemporary coldness. It is a proof of her author's genius, that she is even more intelligible to our age than she was to her own.

At the end of the second volume of the first edition of her history was a notice announcing the immediate appearance of the above-mentioned *Covent-Garden Journal*, a bi-weekly paper, in which Fielding, under the style and title of Sir Alexander Drawcansir, assumed the office of Censor of Great Britain. The first number of this new venture was issued on January the 4th, 1752, and the price was threepence. In plan, and general appearance, it resembled the *Jacobite's Journal*, consisting mainly of an introductory Essay, paragraphs of current news, often accompanied by pointed editorial comment, miscellaneous articles, and advertisements. One of the features of the earlier numbers was a burlesque, but not very successful, Journal of the present Paper War, which speedily involved the author in actual hostilities with the notorious quack and adventurer Dr. John Hill, who for some time had been publishing certain impudent lucubrations in the *London Daily Advertiser* under the heading of *The Inspector;* and also with Smollett, whom he (Fielding) had ridiculed in his second number, perhaps on account of that little paragraph in the first edition of *Peregrine Pickle*, to which reference was made in an earlier chapter. Smollett, always irritable and combative, retorted by a needlessly coarse and venomous pamphlet, in which, under the name of "Habbakkuk Hilding, Justice, Dealer and Chapman," Fielding was attacked with indescribable brutality. Another, and seemingly unprovoked, adversary whom the *Journal of the War* brought upon him was Bonnel Thornton, after-

M

wards joint-author with George Colman of the *Connoisseur*, who, in a production styled *Have at you All ; or, The
Drury Lane Journal,* lampooned Sir Alexander with
remarkable rancour and assiduity. Mr. Lawrence has
treated these "quarrels of authors" at some length ; and
they also have some record in the curious collections of
the elder Disraeli. As a general rule, Fielding was far
less personal and much more scrupulous in his choice of
weapons than those who assailed him ; but the conflict
was an undignified one, and, as Scott has justly said,
"neither party would obtain honour by an inquiry into
the cause or conduct of its hostilities."

In the enumeration of Fielding's works it is somewhat difficult (if due proportion be observed) to assign
any real importance to efforts like the *Covent-Garden
Journal.* Compared with his novels, they are insigni-
ficant enough. But even the worst work of such a man
is notable in its way; and Fielding's contributions to
the *Journal* are by no means to be despised. They are
shrewd lay sermons, often exhibiting much out-of-the-
way erudition, and nearly always distinguished by some
of his personal qualities. In No. 33, on "Profanity,"
there is a character-sketch which, for vigour and vitality,
is worthy of his best days; and there is also a very
thoughtful paper on "Reading," containing a kindly
reference to "the ingenious Author of *Clarissa*," which
should have mollified that implacable moralist. In
this essay it is curious to notice that, while Fielding
speaks with due admiration of Shakespeare and Molière,
Lucian, Cervantes, and Swift, he condemns Rabelais
and Aristophanes, although in the invocation already
quoted from *Tom Jones,* he had included both these

authors among the models he admired. Another paper
in the *Covent - Garden Journal* is especially interesting
because it affords a clue to a project of Fielding's which
unfortunately remained a project. This was a Translation of the works of Lucian, to be undertaken in conjunction with his old colleague, the Rev. William
Young. Proposals were advertised, and the enterprise
was duly heralded by a "puff preliminary," in which
Fielding, while abstaining from anything directly concerning his own abilities, observes, "I will only venture
to say, that no Man seems so likely to translate an
Author well, as he who hath formed his Stile upon that
very Author"—a sentence which, taken in connection
with the references to Lucian in *Tom Thumb*, the *Champion* and elsewhere, must be accepted as distinctly auto-
biographic. The last number of the *Covent - Garden
Journal* (No. 72) was issued in November 1752. By this
time Sir Alexander seems to have thoroughly wearied of
his task. With more gravity than usual he takes leave
of letters, begging the Public that they will not henceforth father on him the dulness and scurrility of his
worthy contemporaries ; "since I solemnly declare that
unless in revising my former Works, I have at present
no Intention to hold any further Correspondence with
the gayer Muses."

The labour of conducting the *Covent-Garden Journal*
must have been the more severe in that, during the
whole period of its existence, the editor was vigorously
carrying out his duties as a magistrate. The prison and
political scenes in *Amelia*, which contemporary critics
regarded as redundant, and which even to us are more
curious than essential, testify at once to his growing

interest in reform, and his keen appreciation of the
defects which existed both in the law itself and in the
administration of the law; while the numerous cases
heard before him, and periodically reported in his paper
by his clerk, afford ample evidence of his judicial activity.
How completely he regarded himself (Bathurst and Rigby
notwithstanding) as the servant of the public, may be
gathered from the following regularly repeated notice:—

"To the PUBLIC.

"All Persons who shall for the Future, suffer by Robbers,
Burglars, &c., are desired immediately to bring, or send, the
best Description they can of such Robbers, &c., with the Time
and Place, and Circumstances of the Fact, to Henry Fielding,
Esq.; at his House in Bow Street."

Another instance of his energy in his vocation is to be
found in the little collection of cases entitled *Examples
of the Interposition of Providence, in the Detection and
Punishment of Murder*, published, with Preface and Introduction, in April 1752, and prompted, as advertisement announces, "by the many horrid Murders committed within this last Year." It appeared, as a matter
of fact, only a few days after the execution at Oxford,
for parricide, of the notorious Miss Mary Blandy, and
might be assumed to have a more or less timely intention;
but the purity of Fielding's purpose is placed beyond a
doubt by the fact that he freely distributed it in court
to those whom it seemed calculated to profit.

The only other works of Fielding which precede the
posthumously published *Journal of a Voyage to Lisbon*
are the *Proposal for Making an Effectual Provision for the
Poor*, etc., a pamphlet dedicated to the Right Honble.
Henry Pelham, published in January 1753; and the

Clear State of the Case of Elizabeth Canning, published in
March. The former, which the hitherto unfriendly
Gentleman's patronisingly styles an "excellent piece,"
conceived in a manner which gives "a high idea of his
[the author's] present temper, manners and ability,"
is an elaborate project for the erection, *inter alia*, of a
vast building, of which a plan, "drawn by an Eminent
Hand," was given, to be called the County-house, capable
of containing 5000 inmates, and including work-rooms,
prisons, an infirmary, and other features, the details of
which are too minute to be repeated in these pages, even
if they had received any attention from the Legislature,
which they did not. The latter was Fielding's contribution to the extraordinary judicial puzzle, which
agitated London in 1753-4. It is needless to do more
than recall its outline. On the 29th of January 1753,
one Elizabeth Canning, a domestic servant aged eighteen
or thereabouts, and who had hitherto borne an excellent
character, returned to her mother, having been missing
from the house of her master, a carpenter in Alderman-
bury, since the 1st of the same month. She was half
starved and half clad, and alleged that she had been
abducted, and confined during her absence in a house on
the Hertford Road, from which she had just escaped.
This house she afterwards identified as that of one
Mother Wells, a person of very indifferent reputation.
An ill-favoured old gipsy woman named Mary Squires was
also declared by her to have been the main agent in ill-
using and detaining her. The gipsy, it is true, averred
that at the time of the occurrence she was a hundred and
twenty miles away; but Canning persisted in her statement. Among other people before whom she came was

Fielding, who examined her, as well as a young woman called Virtue Hall, who appeared subsequently as one of Canning's witnesses. Fielding seems to have been strongly impressed by her appearance and her story, and his pamphlet (which was contradicted in every particular by his adversary, John Hill) gives a curious and not very edifying picture of the magisterial procedure of the time. In February, Wells and Squires were tried; Squires was sentenced to death, and Wells to imprisonment and burning in the hand. Then, by the exertions of the Lord Mayor, Sir Crisp Gascoyne, who doubted the justice of the verdict, Squires was respited and pardoned. Forthwith London was split up into Egyptian and Canningite factions; a hailstorm of pamphlets set in; portraits and caricatures of the principal personages were in all the print shops; and, to use Churchill's words,

" —*Betty Canning* was at least,
With *Gascoyne's* help, a six months feast."

In April 1754, however, Fate so far prevailed against her that she herself, in turn, was tried for perjury. Thirty-six witnesses swore that Squires had been in Dorsetshire; twenty-six that she had been seen in Middlesex. After some hesitation, quite of a piece with the rest of the proceedings, the jury found Canning guilty; and she was transported for seven years. At the end of her sentence she returned to England to receive a legacy of £500, which had been left her by an enthusiastic old lady of Newington-green. Her "case" is full of the most inexplicable contradictions; and it occupies in the *State Trials* some four hundred and twenty closely-printed pages of the most curious and picturesque eighteenth-century details.   But how, from the 1st of January 1753 to the 29th of the same month, Elizabeth Canning really did manage to spend her time is a secret that, to this day, remains undivulged.

CHAPTER VII.

IN March 1753, when Fielding published his pamphlet on Elizabeth Canning, his life was plainly drawing to a close. His energies indeed were unabated, as may be gathered from a brief record in the *Gentleman's* for that month, describing his judicial raid, at four in the morning, upon a gaming-room, where he suspected certain highwaymen to be assembled. But his body was enfeebled by disease, and he knew he could not look for length of days. He had lived not long, but much; he had seen in little space, as the motto to *Tom Jones* announced, "the manners of many men;" and now that, prematurely, the inevitable hour approached, he called Cicero and Horace to his aid, and prepared to meet his fate with philosophic fortitude. Between

> "*Quem fors dierum cunque dabit, lucro*
> *Appone,*"

and

> "*Grata superveniet, quæ non sperabitur, hora,*

he tells us, in his too-little-consulted *Proposal for the Poor*, he had schooled himself to regard events with equanimity, striving above all, in what remained to him of

life, to perform the duties of his office efficiently, and
solicitous only for those he must leave behind him.
Henceforward his literary efforts should be mainly
philanthropic and practical, not without the hope that,
if successful, they might be the means of securing some
provision for his family. Of fiction he had taken formal
leave in the trial of *Amelia;* and of lighter writing
generally in the last paper of the *Covent-Garden Journal.*
But, it we may trust his Introduction, the amount of
work he had done for this poor-law project must have
been enormous, for he had read and considered all the
laws upon the subject, as well as everything that had
been written on it since the days of Elizabeth, yet he
speaks nevertheless as one over whose head the sword
had all the while been impending :—

" The Attempt, indeed, is such, that the Want of Success
can scarce be called a Disappointment, tho' I shall have lost
much Time, and misemployed much Pains ; and what is
above all, shall miss the Pleasure of thinking that in the
Decline of my Health and Life, I have conferred a great and
lasting Benefit on my Country."

In words still more resigned and dignified, he concludes the book :—

His enemies, he says, will no doubt " discover, that instead
of intending a Provision for the Poor, I have been carving
out one for myself,[1] and have very cunningly projected to
build myself a fine House at the Expence of the Public.
This would be to act in direct Opposition to the Advice of
my above Master [*i.e.* Horace] ; it would be indeed

Struere domos immemor sepulchri.

Those who do not know me, may believe this ; but those

---

[1] Presumably as Governor of the proposed County-house.

who do, will hardly be so deceived by that Chearfulness
which was always natural to me ; and which, I thank God,
my Conscience doth not reprove me for, to imagine that I
am not sensible of my declining Constitution. . . . Ambition
or Avarice can no longer raise a Hope, or dictate any Scheme
to me, who have no further Design than to pass my short
Remainder of Life in some Degree of Ease, and barely to
preserve my Family from being the Objects of any such
Laws as I have here proposed."

With the exception of the above, and kindred passages quoted from the Prefaces to the *Miscellanies* and
the Plays, the preceding pages, as the reader has no
doubt observed, contain little of a purely autobiographical
character. Moreover, the anecdotes related of Fielding
by Murphy and others have not always been of such a
nature as to inspire implicit confidence in their accuracy,
while of the very few letters that have been referred to,
none have any of those intimate and familiar touches
which reveal the individuality of the writer. But from
the middle of 1753 up to a short time before his death,
Fielding has himself related the story of his life, in one
of the most unfeigned and touching little tracts in our
own or any other literature. The only thing which, at the
moment, suggests itself for comparison with the *Journal
of a Voyage to Lisbon* is the letter and dedication which
Fielding's predecessor, Cervantes, prefixes to his last
romance of *Persiles and Sigismunda*. In each case the
words are animated by the same uncomplaining kindli-
ness—the same gallant and indomitable spirit ; in each
case the writer is a dying man. Cervantes survived
the date of his letter to the Conde de Lemos but three
days ; and the *Journal*, says Fielding's editor (probably
his brother John), was "finished almost at the same

period with life." It was written, from its author's account, in those moments of the voyage when, his womankind being sea-sick, and the crew wholly absorbed in working the ship, he was thrown upon his own resources, and compelled to employ his pen to while away the time. The Preface, and perhaps the Introduction, were added after his arrival at Lisbon, in the brief period before his death. The former is a semi-humorous apology for voyage-writing; the latter gives an account of the circumstances which led to this, his last expedition in search of health.

At the beginning of August 1753, Fielding tells us, having taken the Duke of Portland's medicine[1] for near a year, "the effects of which had been the carrying off the symptoms of a lingering imperfect gout," Mr. Ranby, the King's Sergeant-Surgeon[2] (to whom complimentary reference had been made in the Man of the Hill's story in *Tom Jones*), with other able physicians, advised him "to go immediately to Bath." He accordingly engaged lodgings, and prepared to leave town forthwith. While he was making ready for his departure, and was "almost fatigued to death with several long examinations, relating to five different murders, all committed within the space of a week, by different gangs of street robbers," he received a message from the Duke of Newcastle, afterwards Premier, through that Mr. Carrington whom Walpole calls "the cleverest of all ministerial terriers," requesting his attendance in Lincoln's-Inn

---

[1] A popular eighteenth-century gout-powder, but as old as Galen. The receipt for it is given in the *Gentleman's Magazine*, vol. xxiii., 579.

[2] Mr. Ranby was also the friend of Hogarth, who etched his house at Chiswick.

Fields (Newcastle House). Being lame, and greatly over-taxed, Fielding excused himself. But the Duke sent Mr. Carrington again next day, and Fielding with great difficulty obeyed the summons. After waiting some three hours in the antechamber (no unusual feature, as Lord Chesterfield informs us, of the Newcastle audiences), a gentleman was deputed to consult him as to the devising of a plan for putting an immediate end to the murders and robberies which had become so common. This, although the visit cost him "a severe cold," Fielding at once undertook. A proposal was speedily drawn out and submitted to the Privy Council. Its essential features were the employment of a known informer, and the provision of funds for that purpose.

By the time this scheme was finally approved, Fielding's disorder had "turned to a deep jaundice," in which case the Bath waters were generally regarded as "almost infallible." But his eager desire to break up "this gang of villains and cut-throats" delayed him in London ; and a day or two after he had received a portion of the stipulated grant, (which portion, it seems, took several weeks in arriving), the whole body were entirely dispersed,— "seven of them were in actual custody, and the rest driven, some out of town, and others out of the kingdom." In examining them, however, and in taking depositions, which often occupied whole days and sometimes nights, although he had the satisfaction of knowing that during the dark months of November and December the metropolis enjoyed complete immunity from murder and robbery, his own health was "reduced to the last extremity."

"Mine (he says) was now no longer what is called a

Bath case," nor, if it had been, could his strength have
sustained the "intolerable fatigue" of the journey
thither. He accordingly gave up his Bath lodgings,
which he had hitherto retained, and went into the
country "in a very weak and deplorable condition."
He was suffering from jaundice, dropsy, and asthma,
under which combination of diseases his body was "so
entirely emaciated, that it had lost all its muscular flesh."
He had begun with reason "to look on his case as
desperate," and might fairly have regarded himself as
voluntarily sacrificed to the good of the public. But he
is far too honest to assign his action to philanthropy
alone. His chief object (he owns) had been, if possible,
to secure some provision for his family in the event of
his death. Not being a "trading justice,"—that is, a
justice who took bribes from suitors, like Justice
Thrasher in *Amelia*, or Justice Squeez'um in the *Coffee
House Politician*,—his post at Bow Street had scarcely
been a lucrative one. "By composing, instead of in-
flaming, the quarrels of porters and beggars (which I
blush when I say hath not been universally practised)
and by refusing to take a shilling from a man who most
undoubtedly would not have had another left, I had
reduced an income of about 500*l* a year of the dirtiest
money upon earth to little more than 300*l*, a considerable proportion of which remained with my clerk."
Besides the residue of his justice's fees, he had also, he
informs us, a yearly pension from the Government, "out
of the public service-money," but the amount is not stated.
The rest of his means, as far as can be ascertained,
were derived from his literary labours. To a man of his
lavish disposition, and with the claims of a family upon

him, this could scarcely have been a competence; and if, as appears not very clearly from a note in the *Journal*, he now resigned his office to his half-brother, who had long been his assistant, his private affairs at the beginning of the winter of 1753-54 must, as he says, have "had but a gloomy aspect." In the event of his death his wife and children could have no hope except from some acknowledgment by the Government of his past services.

Meanwhile his diseases were slowly gaining ground. The terrible winter of 1753-54, which, from the weather record in the *Gentleman's*, seems, with small intermission, to have been prolonged far into April, was especially trying to asthmatic patients, and consequently wholly against him. In February he returned to town, and put himself under the care of the notorious Dr. Joshua Ward of Pall Mall, by whom he was treated and tapped for dropsy.[1] He was at his worst, he says, "on that memorable day when the public lost Mr. Pelham (March 6th);" but from this time, he began, under Ward's medicines, to acquire "some little degree of strength," although his dropsy increased. With May came the long-delayed spring, and he moved to Fordhook,[2] a "little house" belonging to him at Ealing, the air of which place then enjoyed a considerable reputation, being reckoned the best in Middlesex,

[1] Ward appears in Hogarth's *Consultation of Physicians*, 1736, and in Pope—"Ward try'd on Puppies, and the Poor, his Drop." He was a quack, but must have possessed considerable ability. Bolingbroke wished Pope to consult him in 1744; and he attended George II. There is an account of him in Nichols's *Genuine Works of Hogarth*, i. 89.

[2] It lay on the Uxbridge Road, a little beyond Acton, and nearly opposite the present Ealing Common Station of the Metropolitan District Railway. The site is now occupied by a larger house bearing the same name, belonging to Captain Tyrrell.

" and far superior to that of Kensington Gravel-Pits."
Here a re-perusal of Bishop Berkeley's *Siris*, which had
been recalled to his memory by Mrs. Charlotte Lennox,
" the inimitable author of the *Female Quixote*," set him
drinking tar-water with apparent good effect, except as far
as his chief ailment was concerned.   The applications of
the trocar became more frequent : the summer, if summer
it could be called, was " mouldering away ; " and winter,
with all its danger to an invalid, was drawing on apace.
Nothing seemed hopeful but removal to a warmer climate.
Aix in Provence was at first thought of, but the idea was
abandoned on account of the difficulties of the journey.
Lisbon, where Doddridge had died three years before,
was then chosen ; a passage in a vessel trading to the
port was engaged for the sick man, his wife, daughter,
and two servants ; and after some delays they started.
At this point the actual *Journal* begins with a well-
remembered entry :—

" *Wednesday, June 26th*, 1754.—On this day, the most
melancholy sun I had ever beheld arose, and found me awake
at my house at Fordhook.   By the light of this sun, I was, in
my own opinion, last to behold and take leave of some of
those creatures on whom I doated with a mother-like fondness,
guided by nature and passion, and uncured and unhardened
by all the doctrine of that philosophical school where I had
learnt to bear pains and to despise death.

" In this situation, as I could not conquer nature, I
submitted entirely to her, and she made as great a fool of
me as she had ever done of any woman whatsoever : under
pretence of giving me leave to enjoy, she drew me to suffer
the company of my little ones, during eight hours ; and I
doubt not whether, in that time, I did not undergo more
than in all my distemper.

" At twelve precisely my coach was at the door, which
was no sooner told me than I kiss'd my children round, and

went into it with some little resolution. My wife, who behaved more like a heroine and philosopher, tho' at the same time the tenderest mother in the world, and my eldest daughter, followed me ; some friends went with us, and others here took their leave ; and I heard my behaviour applauded, with many murmurs and praises to which I well knew I had no title ; as all other such philosophers may, if they have any modesty, confess on the like occasions."

Two hours later the party reached Rotherhithe. Here, with the kindly assistance of his and Hogarth's friend, Mr. Saunders Welch, High Constable of Holborn, the sick man, who, at this time, "had no use of his limbs," was carried to a boat, and hoisted in a chair over the ship's side. This latter journey, far more fatiguing to the sufferer than the twelve miles ride which he had previously undergone, was not rendered more easy to bear by the jests of the watermen and sailors, to whom his ghastly, death-stricken countenance seemed matter for merriment; and he was greatly rejoiced to find himself safely seated in the cabin. The voyage, however, already more than once deferred, was not yet to begin. Wednesday, being King's Proclamation Day, the vessel could not be cleared at the Custom House; and on Thursday the skipper announced that he should not set out until Saturday. As Fielding's complaint was again becoming troublesome, and no surgeon was available on board, he sent for his friend, the famous anatomist, Mr. Hunter, of Covent Garden,[1] by whom he was tapped, to his own relief, and the admiration of the simple sea-captain, who (he writes) was greatly impressed by "the heroic constancy, with which I had

[1] This must have been William Hunter, for in 1754 his more distinguished brother John had not yet become celebrated.

borne an operation that is attended with scarce any
degree of pain." On Sunday the vessel dropped down
to Gravesend, where, on the next day, Mr. Welch,
who until then had attended them, took his leave; and,
Fielding, relieved by the trocar of any immediate apprehensions of discomfort, might, in spite of his forlorn
case, have been fairly at ease. He had a new concern,
however, in the state of Mrs. Fielding, who was in
agony with toothache, which successive operators failed
to relieve; and there is an unconsciously touching
little picture of the sick man and his skipper, who was
deaf, sitting silently over "a small bowl of punch" in
the narrow cabin, for fear of waking the pain-worn
sleeper in the adjoining state-room. Of his second wife,
as may be gathered from the opening words of the
Journal, Fielding always speaks with the warmest affection and gratitude. Elsewhere, recording a storm off
the Isle of Wight, he says, "My dear wife and child
must pardon me, if what I did not conceive to be any
great evil to myself, I was not much terrified with the
thoughts of happening to them: in truth, I have often
thought they are both too good, and too gentle, to be
trusted to the power of any man." With what a tenacity
of courtesy he treated the whilom Mary Daniel may be
gathered from the following vignette of insolence in
office, which can be taken as a set-off to the malicious
tattle of Walpole :—

"Soon after their departure [*i.e.* Mr. Welch and a com-
panion], our cabin, where my wife and I were sitting together,
was visited by two ruffians, whose appearance greatly corre-
sponded with that of the sheriff's, or rather the knight-
marshal's bailiffs. One of these, especially, who seemed to
affect a more than ordinary degree of rudeness and insolence,

N

came in without any kind of ceremony, with a broad gold lace upon his hat, which was cocked with much military fierceness on his head. An inkhorn at his button-hole, and some papers in his hand, sufficiently assured me what he was, and I asked him if he and his companions were not custom-house officers ; he answered with sufficient dignity that they were, as an information which he seemed to consider would strike the hearer with awe, and suppress all further inquiry ; but on the contrary I proceeded to ask of what rank he was in the Custom house, and receiving an answer from his companion, as I remember, that the gentleman was a riding surveyor ; I replied, that he might be a riding surveyor, but could be no gentleman, for that none who had any title to that denomination would break into the presence of a lady, without any apology, or even moving his hat. He then took his covering from his head, and laid it on the table, saying, he asked pardon, and blamed the mate, who should, he said, have informed him if any persons of distinction were below. I told him he might guess from our appearance (which, perhaps, was rather more than could be said with the strictest adherence to truth) that he was before a gentleman and lady, which should teach him to be very civil in his behaviour, tho' we should not happen to be of the number whom the world calls people of fashion and distinction. However, I said, that as he seemed sensible of his error, and had asked pardon, the lady would permit him to put his hat on again, if he chose it. This he refused with some degree of surliness, and failed not to convince me that, if I should condescend to become more gentle, he would soon grow more rude."

The date of this occurrence was July the 1st. On the evening of the same day they weighed anchor and managed to reach the Nore. For more than a week they were wind-bound in the Downs, but on the 11th they anchored off Ryde, from which place, on the next morning, Fielding despatched the following letter to his brother. Besides giving the name of the captain and

the ship, which are carefully suppressed in the *Journal*,[1]
it is especially interesting as being the last letter written
by Fielding of which we have any knowledge :—

> " On board the Queen of Portugal, Richd Veal at
> anchor on the Mother Bank, off Ryde, to the
> Care of the Post Master of Portsmouth—this is
> my Date and y^r Direction.
>
> July 12 1754.
>
> " Dear Jack, After receiving that agreeable Lre from
> Messrs. Fielding and Co., we weighed on monday morning
> and sailed from Deal to the Westward   Four Days long but
> inconceivably pleasant Passage brought us yesterday to an
> Anchor on the Mother Bank, on the Back of the Isle of
> Wight, where we had last Night in Safety the Pleasure of
> hearing the Winds roar over our Heads in as violent a Tem-
> pest as I have known, and where my only Consideration
> were the Fears which must possess any Friend of ours, (if
> there is happily any such) who really makes our Wellbeing
> the Object of his Concern especially if such Friend should be
> totally inexperienced in Sea Affairs.   I therefore beg that on
> the Day you receive this Mrs Daniel[2] may know that we are
> just risen from Breakfast in Health and Spirits this twelfth
> Instant at 9 in the morning.   Our Voyage hath proved fruit-
> ful in Adventures all which being to be written in the Book,
> you must postpone y^r Curiosity   As the Incidents which

---

[1] Probably this was intentional. Notwithstanding the statement in the "Dedication to the Public" that the text is given
"as it came from the hands of the author," the *Journal*, in the
first issue of 1755, seems to have been considerably "edited."
"Mrs. Francis" (the Ryde landlady) is there called "Mrs. Hum-
phrys," and the portrait of the military coxcomb, together with
some particulars of Fielding's visit to the Duke of Newcastle, and
other details, are wholly omitted.

[2] It will be remembered that the maiden-name of Fielding's
second wife, as given in the Register of St. Bene't's, was Mary
Daniel. "Mrs. Daniel" was therefore, in all probability, Fielding's mother-in-law; and it may reasonably be assumed that she
had remained in charge of the little family at Fordhock.

fall under y^r Cognizance will possibly be consigned to
Oblivion, do give them to us as they pass. Tell y^r Neigh-
bour I am much obliged to him for recommending me to the
Care of a most able and experienced Seaman to whom other
Captains seem to pay such Deference that they attend and
watch his Motions, and think themselves only safe when
they act under his Direction and Example. Our Ship in
Truth seems to give Laws on the Water with as much
Authority and Superiority as you Dispense Laws to the
Public and Examples to y^r Brethren in Commission. Please
to direct y^r Answer to me on Board as in the Date, if gone
to be returned, and then send it by the Post and Pacquet to
Lisbon to

" Y^r affec^t Brother

" H. FIELDING

" To John Fielding Esq. at his House in
     Bow Street Cov^t Garden London."

As the *Queen of Portugal* did not leave Ryde until
the 23d, it is possible that Fielding received a reply.
During the remainder of this desultory voyage he continued to beguile his solitary hours—hours of which
we are left to imagine the physical torture and mono-
tony, for he says but little of himself—by jottings
and notes of the, for the most part, trivial accidents of
his progress. That happy cheerfulness, of which he
spoke in the *Proposal for the Poor*, had not yet deserted
him; and there are moments when he seems rather
on a pleasure-trip than a forlorn pilgrimage in search
of health. At Ryde, where, for change of air, he went
ashore, he chronicles, after many discomforts from
the most disobliging of landladies (let the name of
Mrs. Francis go down to posterity!), "the best, the
pleasantest, and the merriest meal, [in a barn] with more
appetite, more real, solid luxury, and more festivity, than
was ever seen in an entertainment at White's." At

Torbay, he expatiates upon the merits and flavour of the
John Dory, a specimen of which "gloriously regaled"
the party, and furnished him with a pretext for a dis-
sertation on the London Fish Supply.   Another page he
devotes to commendation of the excellent *Vinum Pomonæ*,
or Southam cyder, supplied by "Mr. Giles Leverance of
Cheeshurst, near Dartmouth in Devon," of which, for
the sum of five pounds ten shillings, he extravagantly
purchases three hogsheads, one for himself, and the
others as presents for friends, among whom no doubt was
kindly Mr. Welch.   Here and there he sketches, with
but little abatement of his earlier gaiety and vigour, the
human nature around him.   Of the objectionable Ryde
landlady and her husband there are portraits not much
inferior to those of the Tow-wouses in *Joseph Andrews*,
while the military fop, who visits his uncle the captain
off Spithead, is drawn with all the insight which depicted
the vagaries of Ensign Northerton, whom indeed the real
hero of the *Journal* not a little resembles.   The best
character sketch, however, in the whole is that of Captain
Richard Veal himself (one almost feels inclined to wonder
whether he was in any way related to the worthy lady
whose apparition visited Mrs. Bargrave at Canterbury !),
but it is of necessity somewhat dispersed.   It has also an
additional attraction, because, if we remember rightly, it
is Fielding's sole excursion into the domain of Smollett.
The rough old sea-dog of the Haddock and Vernon period,
who had been a privateer; and who still, as skipper of a
merchant-man, when he visits a friend or gallants the
ladies, decorates himself with a scarlet coat, cockade, and
sword ; who gives vent to a kind of Irish howl when his
favourite kitten is suffocated under a feather bed ; and

falls abjectly on his knees when threatened with the dreadful name of Law, is a character which, in its surly good-humour and sensitive dignity, might easily, under more favourable circumstances, have grown into an individuality, if not equal to that of Squire Western, at least on a level with Partridge or Colonel Bath. There are numbers of minute touches—as, for example, his mistaking "a lion" for "Elias" when he reads prayers to the ship's company; and his quaint asseverations when exercised by the inconstancy of the wind—which show how closely Fielding studied his deaf companion. But it would occupy too large a space to examine the *Journal* more in detail. It is sufficient to say that after some further delays from wind and tide, the travellers sailed up the Tagus. Here, having undergone the usual quarantine and custom-house obstruction, they landed, and Fielding's penultimate words record a good supper at Lisbon, "for which we were as well charged, as if the bill had been made on the Bath Road, between Newbury and London." The book ends with a line from the poet whom, in the *Proposal for the Poor*, he had called his master :—

"—*hic finis chartæque viæque.*"

Two months afterwards he died at Lisbon, on the 8th of October, in the forty-eighth year of his age.

He was buried on the hillside in the centre of the beautiful English cemetery, which faces the great Basilica of the Heart of Jesus, otherwise known as the Church of the Estrella. Here, in a leafy spot where the nightingales fill the still air with song, and watched by those secular cypresses from which the place takes its Portuguese name of *Os Cyprestes*, lies all that was mortal of

him whom Scott called the "Father of the English
Novel." His first tomb, which Wraxall found in 1772,
"nearly concealed by weeds and nettles," was erected by
the English factory, in consequence mainly—as it seems
—of a proposal made by an enthusiastic Chevalier de
Meyrionnet, to provide one (with an epitaph) at his
own expense. That now existing was substituted in
1830, by the exertions of the Rev. Christopher Neville,
British Chaplain at Lisbon. It is a heavy sarco-
phagus, resting upon a large base, and surmounted by
just such another urn and flame as that on Hogarth's
Tomb at Chiswick. On the front is a long Latin inscription; on the back the better-known words :—

> LUGET BRITANNIA GREMIO NON DARI
> FOVERE NATUM.[1]

It is to this last memorial that the late George Borrow
referred in his *Bible in Spain :*—

"Let travellers devote one entire morning to inspecting
the Arcos and the Mai das agoas, after which they may
repair to the English church and cemetery, Père-la-chaise in
miniature, where, if they be of England, they may well be
excused if they kiss the cold tomb, as I did, of the author of
"Amelia," the most singular genius which their island ever
produced, whose works it has long been the fashion to abuse
in public and to read in secret."

Borrow's book was first published in 1843. Of late
years the tomb had been somewhat neglected; but
from a communication in the *Athenæum* of May 1879,
it appears that it had then been recently cleaned, and

---

[1] The fifth word is generally given as "datum." But the above
version, which has been verified at Lisbon, may be accepted as
correct.

the inscriptions restored, by order of the present
chaplain, the Rev. Godfrey Pope.

There is but one authentic portrait of Henry Fielding.
This is the pen-and-ink sketch drawn from memory by
Hogarth, long after Fielding's death, to serve as a frontispiece for Murphy's edition of his works. It was engraved
in *facsimile* by James Basire, with such success that
the artist is said to have mistaken an impression of the
plate (without its emblematic border) for his own drawing. Hogarth's sketch is the sole source of all the
portraits, more or less "romanced," which are prefixed
to editions of Fielding; and also, there is good reason
to suspect, of the dubious little miniature, still in possession of his descendants, which figures in Hutchins's
History of Dorset and elsewhere. More than one account
has been given of the way in which the drawing was
produced. The most effective, and, unfortunately, the
most popular, version has, of course, been selected by
Murphy. In this he tells us that Hogarth, being unable to recall his dead friend's features, had recourse
to a profile cut in paper by a lady, who possessed the
happy talent which Pope ascribes to Lady Burlington.
Her name, which is given in Nichols, was Margaret
Collier, and she was possibly the identical Miss Collier who figures in Richardson's *Correspondence*. Setting aside the fact that, as Hogarth's eye-memory was
phenomenal, this story is highly improbable, it was expressly contradicted by George Steevens in 1781, and by
John Ireland in 1798, both of whom, from their relations
with Hogarth's family, were likely to be credibly informed. Steevens, after referring to Murphy's fable,
says in the *Biographical Anecdotes of William Hogarth*, "I

am assured that our artist began and finished the head
in the presence of his wife and another lady. He had
no assistance but from his own memory, which, on such
occasions, was remarkably tenacious." Ireland, in his
Hogarth Illustrated, gives us as the simple fact the following:—"Hogarth being told, after his friend's death,
that a portrait was wanted as a frontispiece to his works,
sketched this from memory." According to the inscription on Basire's plate, it represents Fielding at the age
of forty-eight, or in the year of his death. This, however, can only mean that it represents him as Hogarth
had last seen him. But long before he died, disease had
greatly altered his appearance ; and he must have been
little more than the shadow of the handsome Harry
Fielding, who wrote farces for Mrs. Clive, and heard the
chimes at midnight. As he himself says in the *Voyage
to Lisbon*, he had lost his teeth, and the consequent fall-
ing-in of the lips is plainly perceptible in the profile.
The shape of the Roman nose, which Colonel James in
Amelia irreverently styled a "proboscis," would, however, remain unaltered, and it is still possible to divine a
curl, half humorous, half ironic, in the short upper lip.
The eye, apparently, was dark and deep-set. Oddly
enough, the chin, to the length of which he had himself
referred in the *Champion*, does not appear abnormal.[1]

[1] In the bust of Fielding which Miss Margaret Thomas has
been commissioned by Mr. R. A. Kinglake to execute for the
Somerset Valhalla, the Shire-Hall at Taunton, these points have
been carefully considered ; and the sculptor has succeeded in pro-
ducing a work which, while it suggests the mingling of humour and
dignity that is Fielding's chief characteristic, is also generally faithful to Hogarth's indications. From these, indeed, it is impossible
to deviate. Not only is his portrait unique ; but (and this is con-

Beyond the fact that he was above six feet in height, and, until the gout had broken his constitution, unusually robust, Murphy adds nothing further to our idea of his personal appearance.

That other picture of his character, traced and retraced (often with much exaggeration of outline), is so familiar in English literature, that it cannot now be materially altered or amended. Yet it is impossible not to wish that it were derived from some less prejudiced or more trustworthy witnesses than those who have spoken,— say, for example, from Lyttelton or Allen. There are always signs that Walpole's malice, and Smollett's animosity, and the rancour of Richardson, have had too much to do with the representation ; and even Murphy and Lady Mary are scarcely persons whom one would select as ideal biographers. The latter is probably right in comparing her cousin to Sir Richard Steele. Both were generous, kindly, brave, and sensitive ; both were improvident ; both loved women and little children ; both sinned often, and had their moments of sincere repentance ; to both was given that irrepressible hopefulness, and full delight of being which forgets to-morrow in to-day. That Henry Fielding was wild and reckless in his youth it would be idle to contest ;—indeed it is an intelligible, if not a necessary, consequence of his physique and his temperament. But it is not fair to speak of him as if his youth lasted for ever. "Critics and biographers," says Mr. Leslie Stephen, "have dwelt far too exclusively upon the uglier side of his Bohemian life ;" and Fielding himself, in the *Jacobite's Journal*, complains sadly

firmed by Ireland and Steevens) it was admitted to be like Fielding by Fielding's friends.

that his enemies have traced his impeachment "even to his boyish Years." That he who was prodigal as a lad was prodigal as a man may be conceded; that he who was sanguine at twenty would be sanguine at forty (although this is less defensible) may also be allowed. But, if we press for "better assurance than Bardolph," there is absolutely no good evidence that Fielding's career after his marriage materially differed from that of other men struggling for a livelihood, hampered with ill-health, and exposed to all the shifts and humiliations of necessity. If any portrait of him is to be handed down to posterity, let it be the last rather than the first; —not the Fielding of the green-room and the tavern— of Covent Garden frolics and "modern conversations;" but the energetic magistrate, the tender husband and father, the kindly host of his poorer friends, the practical philanthropist, the patient and magnanimous hero of the *Voyage to Lisbon*. If these things be remembered, it will seem of minor importance that to his dying day he never knew the value of money, or that he forgot his troubles over a chicken and champagne. And even his improvidence was not without its excusable side. Once—so runs the legend—Andrew Millar made him an advance to meet the claims of an importunate tax-gatherer. Carrying it home, he met a friend, in even worse straits than his own; and the money changed hands. When the tax-gatherer arrived there was nothing but the answer—"Friendship has called for the money and had it; let the collector call again." Justice, it is needless to say, was satisfied by a second advance from the bookseller. But who shall condemn the man of whom such a story can be told?

The literary work of Fielding is so inextricably inter-
woven with what is known of his life that most of it has
been examined in the course of the foregoing narrative.
What remains to be said is chiefly in summary of what
has been said already. As a dramatist he has no eminence ; and though his plays do not deserve the sweeping
condemnation with which Macaulay once spoke of them
in the House of Commons, they are not likely to attract
any critics but those for whom the inferior efforts of a
great genius possess a morbid fascination. Some of them
serve, in a measure, to illustrate his career ; others contain
hints and situations which he afterwards worked into his
novels ; but the only ones that possess real stage qualities
are those which he borrowed from Regnard and Molière.
Don Quixote in England, Pasquin, the *Historical Register,*
can claim no present consideration commensurate with
that which they received as contemporary satires, and
their interest is mainly antiquarian ; while *Tom Thumb*
and the *Covent-Garden Tragedy,* the former of which would
make the reputation of a smaller man, can scarcely hope
to be remembered beside *Amelia* or *Jonathan Wild.*
Nor can it be admitted that, as a periodical writer,
Fielding was at his best. In spite of effective passages,
his essays remain far below the work of the great
Augustans, and are not above the level of many of
their less illustrious imitators. That instinct of popular
selection, which retains a faint hold upon the *Rambler,*
the *Adventurer,* the *World,* and the *Connoisseur,* or at
least consents to give them honourable interment as
" British Essayists" in a secluded corner of the shelves,
has made no pretence to any preservation, or even any
winnowing, of the *Champion* and the *True Patriot.* Field-

ing's papers are learned and ingenious; they are frequently humorous ; they are often earnest ; but it must
be a loiterer in literature who, in these days, except for
antiquarian or biographical purposes, can honestly find it
worth while to consult them. His pamphlets and projects
are more valuable, if only that they prove him to have
looked curiously and sagaciously at social and political
problems, and to have striven, as far as in him lay, to set
the crooked straight. Their import, to-day, is chiefly
that of links in a chain—of contributions to a progressive
literature which has travelled into regions unforeseen by
the author of the *Proposal for the Poor*, and the *Inquiry
into the Causes of the late Increase of Robbers*. As such, they
have their place in that library of Political Economy of
which Mr. M'Culloch has catalogued the riches. It is
not, however, by his pamphlets, his essays, or his plays
that Fielding is really memorable ; it is by his triad of
novels, and the surpassing study in irony of *Jonathan
Wild*. In *Joseph Andreus* we have the first sprightly
runnings of a genius that, after much uncertainty, had
at last found its fitting vein, but was yet doubtful
and undisciplined : in *Tom Jones* the perfect plan has
come, with the perfected method and the assured expression. There is an inevitable loss of that fine way-
wardness which is sometimes the result of untrained
effort, but there is the general gain of order, and the
full production which results of art. The highest point
is reached in *Tom Jones*, which is the earliest definite
and authoritative manifestation of the modern novel.
Its relation to De Foe is that of the vertebrate to the
invertebrate : to Richardson, that of the real to the
ideal—one might almost add, the impossible. It can

be compared to no contemporary English work of its
own kind; and if we seek for its parallel at the time
of publication we must go beyond literature to art—to
the masterpiece of that great pictorial satirist who
was Fielding's friend. In both Fielding and Hogarth
there is the same constructive power, the same rigid
sequence of cause and effect, the same significance of
detail, the same side-light of allusion. Both have the
same hatred of affectation and hypocrisy—the same un-
erring insight into character. Both are equally attracted
by striking contrasts and comic situations; in both there
is the same declared morality of purpose, coupled with
the same sturdy virility of expression. One, it is true,
leaned more strongly to tragedy, the other to comedy.
But if Fielding had painted pictures, it would have been
in the style of the *Marriage à la Mode;* if Hogarth had
written novels, they would have been in the style of *Tom
Jones.* In the gentler and more subdued *Amelia,* with
its tender and womanly central-figure, there is a certain
change of plan, due to altered conditions—it may be,
to an altered philosophy of art. The narrative is less
brisk and animated; the character-painting less broadly
humorous; the philanthropic element more strongly
developed. To trace the influence of these three great
works in succeeding writers would hold us too long. It
may, nevertheless, be safely asserted that there are few
English novels of manners, written since Fielding's day,
which do not descend from him as from their fount and
source; and that more than one of our modern masters
betrays unmistakable signs of a form and fashion studied
minutely from his frank and manly ancestor.

POSTSCRIPT.

A few particulars respecting Fielding's family and posthumous works can scarcely be omitted from the present memoir. It has been stated that by his first wife he had one daughter, the Eleanor Harriot who accompanied him to Lisbon, and survived him, although Mr. Keightley says, but without giving his authority, she did not survive him long. Of his family by Mary Daniel, the eldest son, William, to whose birth reference has already been made, was bred to the law, became a barrister of the Middle Temple eminent as a special pleader, and ultimately a Westminster magistrate. He died in October 1820, at the age of seventy-three. He seems to have shared his father's conversational qualities,[1] and, like him, to have been a strenuous advocate of the poor and unfortunate. Southey, writing from Keswick in 1830 to Sir Egerton Brydges, speaks of a meeting he had in St. James's Park, about 1817, with one of the novelist's sons. "He was then," says Southey, "a fine old man, though visibly shaken by time : he received me in a manner which had much of old courtesy about it, and I looked upon him with great interest for his father's sake." The date, and the fact that William

[1] *Vide* Lockhart's *Life of Scott*, chap. l.

Fielding had had a paralytic stroke, make it almost
certain that this was he; and a further reference by
Southey to his religious opinions is confirmed by the
obituary notice in the *Gentleman's*, which speaks of him
as a worthy and pious man. The names and baptisms
of the remaining children, as supplied for these pages by
the late Colonel Chester, were Mary Amelia, baptized
January 6, 1749 ; Sophia, January 21, 1750 ; Louisa,
December 3, 1752 ; and Allen, April 6, 1754, about a
month before Fielding removed to Ealing. All these
baptisms took place at St. Paul's, Covent Garden, from
the registers of which these particulars were extracted.
The eldest daughter, Mary Amelia, does not appear to
have long survived, for the same registers record her
burial on the 17th December 1749. Allen Fielding
became a clergyman, and died, according to Burke,
in 1823, being then vicar of St. Stephen's, Canterbury.
He left a family of four sons and three daughters. One
of the sons, George, became rector of North Ockendon,
Essex, and married, in 1825, Mary Rebecca, daughter
of Ferdinand Hanbury-Williams, and grandniece of
Fielding's friend and school-fellow Sir Charles. This
lady, who so curiously linked the present and the past,
died not long since at Hereford Square, Brompton, in
her eighty-fifth year. Mrs. Fielding herself (Mary
Daniel) appears to have attained a good old age. Her
death took place at Canterbury on the 11th of March
1802, perhaps in the house of her son Allen, who is
stated by Nichols in his *Leicestershire* to have been
rector in 1803 of St. Cosmus and Damian-in-the-Blean.
After her husband's death, her children were educated
by their uncle John and Ralph Allen, the latter of

whom—says Murphy—made a very liberal annual dona-
tion for that purpose; and (adds Chalmers in a note),
when he died in 1764, bequeathed to the widow and
those of her family then living, the sum of £100 each.

Among Fielding's other connections it is only necessary to speak of his sister Sarah, and his above-mentioned
brother John. Sarah Fielding continued to write; and in
addition to *David Simple*, published the *Governess*, 1749;
a translation of Xenophon's *Memorabilia*; a dramatic
fable called the *Cry*, and some other forgotten books.
During the latter part of her life she lived at Bath,
where she was highly popular, both for her personal
character and her accomplishments. She died in
1768; and her friend, Dr. John Hoadly, who wrote the
verses to the *Rake's Progress*, erected a monument to
her memory in the Abbey Church.

> "Her unaffected Manners, candid Mind,
> Her Heart benevolent, and Soul resign'd;
> Were more her Praise than all she knew or thought
> Though Athens Wisdom to her Sex she taught,"—

says he; but in mere facts the inscription is, as he
modestly styles it, a "deficient Memorial," for she is described as having been born in 1714 instead of 1710,
and as being the second daughter of General *Henry*
instead of General *Edmund* Fielding. John Fielding,
the novelist's half-brother, as already stated, succeeded
him at Bow Street, though the post is sometimes
claimed (on Boswell's authority) for Mr. Welch. The
mistake no doubt arose from the circumstance that
they frequently worked in concert. Previous to his
appointment as a magistrate, John Fielding, in addition to assisting his brother, seems to have been largely

o

concerned in the promotion of that curious enterprise, the "Universal-Register-Office," so often advertised in the *Covent-Garden Journal*. It appears to have been an Estate Office, Lost Property Office, Servants' Registry, Curiosity Shop, and multifarious General Agency. As a magistrate, in spite of his blindness, John Fielding was remarkably energetic, and is reported to have known more than 3000 thieves by their voices alone, and could recognise them when brought into Court. He wrote a description of London and Westminster, as well as some professional and other works. He was knighted in 1761, and died at Brompton Place in 1780. Lyttelton, who had become Sir George in 1751, was raised to the peerage as Baron Lyttelton of Frankley three years after Fielding's death. He died in 1773. In 1760-5 he published his *Dialogues of the Dead*, profanely characterised by Mr. Walpole as "Dead Dialogues." No. 28 of these is a colloquy between "Plutarch, Charon, and a Modern Bookseller," and it contains the following reference to Fielding : —"We have [says Mr. Bookseller] another writer of these imaginary histories, one who has not long since descended to these regions. His name is Fielding ; and his works, as I have heard the best judges say, have a true spirit of comedy, and an exact representation of nature, with fine moral touches. He has not indeed given lessons of pure and consummate virtue, but he has exposed vice and meanness with all the powers of ridicule." It is perhaps excusable that Lawrence, like Roscoe and others, should have attributed this to Lyttelton; but the preface nevertheless assigns it, with two other dialogues, to a "different hand." They were, in fact, the first essays in authorship of that illustrious blue-stocking, Mrs. Elizabeth Montagu.

Fielding's only posthumous works are the *Journal of a Voyage to Lisbon* and the comedy of *The Fathers; or, The Good-Natur'd Man*. The *Journal* was published in February 1755, together with a fragment of a Comment on Bolingbroke's *Essays*, which Mallet had issued in March of the previous year. This fragment must therefore have been begun in the last months of Fielding's life; and, according to Murphy, he made very careful preparation for the work, as attested by long extracts from the Fathers and the leading controversialists, which, after his death, were preserved by his brother. Beyond a passage or two in Richardson's *Correspondence*, and a sneering reference by Walpole to Fielding's "account how his dropsy was treated and teased by an innkeeper's wife in the Isle of Wight," there is nothing to show how the *Journal* was received, still less that it brought any substantial pecuniary relief to "those innocents," to whom reference had been made in the "Dedication." The play was not placed upon the stage until 1778. Its story, which is related in the *Advertisement*, is curious. After it had been set aside in 1742,[1] it seems to have been submitted to Sir Charles Hanbury Williams. Sir Charles was just starting for Russia, as Envoy Extraordinary. Whether the MS. went with him or not is unknown; but it was lost until 1775 or 1776, when it was recovered in a tattered and forlorn condition by Mr. Johnes, M.P. for Cardigan, from a person who entertained a very poor and even contemptuous opinion of its merits. Mr. Johnes thought otherwise. He sent it to Garrick, who at once recognised it as "Harry Fielding's Comedy." Revised and

[1] *Vide* chap. iv. p. 94.

retouched by the actor and Sheridan, it was produced at Drury Lane, as *The Fathers*, with a Prologue and Epilogue by Garrick. For a few nights it was received with interest, and even some flickering enthusiasm. It was then withdrawn; and there is no likelihood that it will ever be revived.

THE END.

Printed by R. & R. CLARK, *Edinburgh.*

For EU product safety concerns, contact us at Calle de José Abascal, 56–1°,
28003 Madrid, Spain or eugpsr@cambridge.org.

www.ingramcontent.com/pod-product-compliance
Ingram Content Group UK Ltd.
Pitfield, Milton Keynes, MK11 3LW, UK
UKHW012346130625
459647UK00009B/584